Stone Bridge Press • Berkeley, California

Wanna see inside?
ナカミル？

CRUISI
ANIME
AN OTAKU GUID
オタク

PATRICK MACIAS   AND

Published by
Stone Bridge Press
P.O. Box 8208
Berkeley, CA 94707
TEL 510-524-8732
sbp@stonebridge.com
www.stonebridge.com

＊

Text © 2004 Patrick Macias
and Tomohiro Machiyama.

Photos, Illustrations, and Maps
© 2004 jaPRESS.

Book Production by jaPRESS.
info@japress.com

10 9 8 7 6 5 4 3 2
2008 2007 2006 2005

ISBN 1-880656-88-4.

Printed in China.

P.8 **INTRODUCTION**

Let's connect picture!

ING THE
E CITY
DE TO NEO TOKYO

ガイド

TOMOHIRO MACHIYAMA

mapP.29

mapP.83

mapP.125

mapP.141

NAKANO BROADWAY

AKIHABARA

Easy navigation!

INTRODUCTION

November 2003, at a TV studio somewhere in Tokyo (Nakano, I think).

I'm hiding behind a piece of plastic wrap as two buxom female wrestlers flop around in a ring filled with yams, eggs, and lotion. Somehow, I've found my way to a taping of the late-night TV show called *The Real Cat Fight*.

As the girls bounce about trying to grab handfuls of increasingly slippery hair, and the male crowd (who come here every week to stalk their favorite wrestlers) cheers, I start to wonder to myself, how the heck did I ever wind up here, what's this all got to do with anime, and how bad will it stain if the plastic wrap lets me down and I get splattered?

Almost a year later, I'm in my apartment in San Francisco writing these words. I can reach out and grasp an "Anime Art Book" for *Mobile Suit Gundam III*, a capsule toy of Robot Junior from *Mazinger Z*, and a DVD compilation of Morning Musume music videos. Then I turn around and look at the rest of my room. It's an enormous mess of videos, DVDs, manga, toys, CDs, and other goods from Japan.

For years, I tried to track down stuff like this as best I could, at US-based "Japantowns," from fan networks, or through mail-order dealers. But like all non-Japanese fans of Japanese pop culture, I longed to visit the fabled, almost mystical Land of the Rising Sun for myself in search of bigger and better scores.

The first time I went to Tokyo was in 1999. The trip was little more than a shopping spree. While I brought back a lot of goods and some fond memories, I never gained much insight about how a place like Akihabara became a geek paradise, or what sort of minds would conceive of an otaku superstore like Mandarake. Heck, I was too busy try-ing to track down an elusive *Space Battleship Yamato III* anime book.

In the winter of 2001, I met

Tomohiro Machiyama. Ten years my senior, he had written several of the anime and *kaiju* (monster) books that used to fuel my dreams of someday going to Japan. He'd even helped coin the modern use of the word "otaku" in his best-selling tome *The Book of Otaku*. Tomo became my *senpai* (Superior) and I his *kohai* (Junior), and we went to Japan.

Tomo was the Virgil to my Dante in a Tokyo-based divine comedy. He delighted in throwing me into bizarre situations that boggled my Western brain. He introduced me to people (interviewed herein) who played roles in various otaku capacities, and he lectured me on the history and nuances of Japanese otaku culture—sometimes until his voice gave out, literally. Soon, I was trying to get my head around concepts like *moe,* singing karaoke with computer hackers, and standing in the presence of fully grown adults who loved plastic model kits more than members of their own family.

After visiting Tokyo with Tomo several more times, I began to feel, on my most recent trip, that some very big changes were afoot. I'd arrived once again to drink deep from the fountain of anime, but it appeared to be drying up. The most popular anime on TV currently is kid's stuff, like *Crayon Shinchan* and *Dragonball Z.* The bulk of mature-themed anime (the kind that ropes in fans from around the world) is shown on late-night television, and followed only by dedicated otaku. Even theatrical anime, like the films of Mamoru Oshii (*The Ghost in the Shell*), are not so profitable. In fact, it could be argued that there hasn't been a "hit" anime since Studio Gainax's *Neon Genesis Evangelion* peaked in 1997.

Yet while the anime industry itself is shrinking, the otaku industries around it are growing bigger and bigger. In the beginning of Katsuhiro Otomo's anime and manga *AKIRA,* Tokyo is destroyed by a powerful psychic blast that triggers World War III. The city that emerges from the dust is christened "Neo-Tokyo." Try to imagine that all over again with anime as the catalyst for the big bang.

For half a century, Japanese animation was confined to television and movie screens. It excelled at imitating reality, exaggerating it, and showing audiences impossible things. Now, in Japan, it is reality that seems to be imitating anime. Pictures or CGI of big-eyed baby-face anime-type girls are smiling everywhere in video games, how-to manuals, pachinko parlors, train ticket machines, and maid cafes, and even in the sex industry.

The more you look around in Japan, the more anime influence you are likely to see. That's because anime is literally everywhere and has transformed Tokyo into an Anime City. And daily life there is stranger, more exciting, and more vital than any anime I've ever seen. Take that *Real Cat Fight* wrestling match for instance.

But be warned, the pace of change in the Anime City is merciless. Comedian Chris Rock might as well have been talking about cultural trends in Tokyo when he said, "Here today, gone today" of the US music industry. As much as we'd like this book to put things in perspective once and for all, it might wind up as just a snapshot of people and places that did their thing, made an impact, and were gone in the blink of an eye. But who knows? Maybe the

Tokyo we've stumbled upon will turn out to be something more permanent: an eternal thought in the mind of Godzilla perhaps.

If you *really are* going to kick down and make the big trip, there are some other investments you'll want to consider. One of them is Kodansha International's indispensable book *Tokyo City Atlas: A Bilingual Guide*. Not a lot of jokes and thrills in there, but it is still a must for getting from point A to point B with a minimum of fuss. You might even want to look into an otaku-friendly tour package from Pop Japan Travel (www.pop japantravel.com), which will prove helpful not only if you want to hit the usual hot spots but also if you want to get a peek inside an animation studio and enjoy seasonal events like Comiket to their fullest.

If you merely want to use this book to fuel some nice daydreams about someday visiting Tokyo, please enjoy it as such. Those can be fun too.

But don't be surprised if you see the influence of anime and manga culture continue to spread into your own backyard.

The odds are, we'll all be living in an Anime City soon, be it Neo Tokyo or someplace else. ∂

Patrick Macias
San Francisco, August 2004

Mondo Tokyo:
OTAKU

In 1989, I wrote a book called *Otaku no Hon (The Book of Otaku)* that helped popularize the word "otaku" in Japan for the first time. The book was a collection of essays about people deeply into anime, dojinshi (fan-made comics), Bishojo ("Beautiful Girl") figures, *yaoi* (male-male love), computers, video games, pro wrestling, and B-class idol singers. It also included analysis and discussion from scholars about these new kinds of cultures

Otaku no Hon became a bestseller. Inspired by it, Toshio Okada, producer of the 1988 seminal anime *Gunbuster*, made another anime in 1992 called *Otaku no Video* that further explored the otaku phenomenon.

Today, the word "otaku" is listed in Japanese dictionaries and is being used around the world among anime fans. But before *Otaku no Hon* was published the term was known only among one's fellow hard-core otaku.

But it was actually six years before my book came out that the word "otaku" was born. In June 1983, an essayist named Akio Nakamori wrote a short column titled "Otaku no Kenkyu" (A Study of Otaku) for the erotic manga magazine *Manga Brikko*.

Nakamori studied a particular kind of driven personality: people who line up in front of theaters all night before the opening of an anime film, people trying to take photos of rarely seen trains only to nearly get run over by them, kids with Coke-bottle glasses who hang around computer stores, men who go to Idol autograph sessions early in the morning to secure a good seat in front, and audiophiles who are extremely uptight about sound quality. These kinds of people were often called maniacs, enthusiastic fans, or (in Japanese) *nekura*, but none of these terms really hit the target.

People needed a new word to integrate these kinds of people into a broader social phenomenon. In the absence of any better ideas, commentators seized upon the word "otaku."

Observers had noted how fans at anime conventions or get-togethers would use the word "otaku" to address each other. When translated into English, "otaku" simply means "you." But whereas in English there is only this all-purpose "you" ("thee" is heard only in sermons), Japan has many "you" equivalents. Which one is used depends on social context, rank, mood, etc. Among all the "you's" in Japan, "otaku" is formal and impersonal. *Taku* means "house," and when combined with the honorific prefix "o"- it literally means "your house," "your side," or "your family." For instance, "you" becomes "otaku" at afternoon tea parties where middle-class housewives regard each other not as individuals but as members of a larger family or lineage. Example: "So, how is your otaku doing?" It helps make the conversation flow easier without the need for personal information.

"Otaku" is a kind of dispassionate and aloof way of referring to another person to his or her face. No wonder Nakamori wrote: "Isn't it creepy to see junior high school kids calling each other 'otaku' at comic and anime conventions?"

How did anime fans begin to use a word that came from housewives? One possible reason is that they were not comfortable with the alternative term for "you": omae. Traditionally, male friends use the first-person ore and the second-person omae. But omae can sound a bit rough to Japanese ears and is properly used only in close relationships and for those at the same or lower rank. It's actually more like "my nigga" than "my buddy." A meek anime fan, reluctant to use such overpowering masculine words, finds the housewife word "otaku" more suited to his and his colleagues' sensibility.

Also, just as housewives will relate to others only as representatives of a family, and not as individuals, anime fans don't want to cross over into each other's personal lives. Information about common interests and hobbies should be the only things exchanged when talking to each other. By calling each other "otaku," personal feelings are off the table; in the fantasy world of anime, this is a sure route to simple communication.

The first recorded usage of "otaku" in the mass media actually came before Akio Nakamori's observations. It popped up in the 1982–83 anime series Super Dimensional Fortress Macross (shown in the USA as Robotech). The fighter–pilot protagonist Hikaru Ichijoe frequently uses "otaku" when addressing others. It seems that the Macross staff, including the scriptwriters, were anime fans themselves and had inadvertently used their own vernacular.

However, because the magazine in which Akio Nakamori had defined the word "otaku" was a little-known porno publication, news about the new usage of the word did not spread far.

Much as I'd like to think that it was my book, Otaku no Hon, that made the word a sensation in 1989, the truth is somewhat different. Tsutomu Miyazaki, a man who kidnapped, raped, and murdered three little girls, was arrested in 1989. Miyazaki was a walking worst-case-scenario otaku. With messy long hair, a pale face, and geeky glasses, he was twenty-seven years old, unemployed, and living with his parents. His room was full of anime videos and Lolicon (Lolita Complex) manga. Because the case was so sensational, many Japanese people began to wonder what kind of lifestyle had created such a monster.

Otaku no Hon had just come out. People connected the dots and came to the conclusion that otaku were dangerous perverts. Otaku suddenly became a social problem. Like Communists or terrorists, the vilified otaku had somehow managed to infiltrate the whole of Japanese society. A mother, worried about her son who was over twenty and without a girlfriend, fainted when she found an erotic manga in his room that showed anime characters being violated. "Otaku bashing" became a new witch hunt.

Otaku even began to despise their own kind. Hardcore otaku who could never have normal lives were called "Itai" (The Painful), and fellow otaku condemned them. Anime otaku were ashamed to be associated with the word "otaku" and stopped using it to address or refer to each other.

The late '80's in Japan was the peak of the Bubble Economy. The ideal man was supposed to be working in finance or for an advertising agency, wearing an Italian double-breasted suit, driving a BMW, exercising at a gym, and enjoying nightlife at upscale discos. On the dark side of this bright and lively Japan were the otaku. But the Bubble Economy in Japan began to burst in 1989, ending the period of high economic growth after World War II and beginning a deep recession that lingers to this day.

As other industries grew

sluggish, only the otaku market kept booming. Anime, manga, and video games became the new favored exports of Japan. Marketers and economists started to research otaku consumers' tendencies and preferences. Academics started researching the psychology of otaku, now considered a model of human beings in a new postmodern society.

Meanwhile, Toshio Okada (remember him?) crossed over from being an anime creator to a social critic. He christened himself the "Ota-King" and started to explain otaku culture in simple words to economists and academics. In a reversal of the events of 1989, otaku were acknowledged as a subculture that Japan could be proud of and learn from.

After all, it was the otaku who, through their purchasing power, supported technological advances in Japan, especially with the consumer electronics and computers they used to store, reproduce, and view their favored products. The idea that otaku somehow hold the key to ending the recession has penetrated

both the corporate world and the highest levels of government.

And one can now say, "I've a little bit of otaku in me" without feeling ashamed. The word "otaku" has acquired a positive connotation, suggesting that a person has his or her own sense of values, is not a snob, has a child's purity and passion, and possesses in-depth knowledge and an uncompromising opinion on his own likes and dislikes. A person minus otaku leanings is assumed to be without uniqueness, originality, or creativity.

A change has happened to the meaning of "otaku," similar to what happened with the once-insulting word "queer." Of course, the negative meaning of "otaku" is still widely used. "Ota," a shortened version of "otaku," is used to ridicule someone or make fun of oneself. An otaku of the idol group Morning Musume, for example, is a "Mo-ota"; an otaku of Gundam is "Gun-ota." What kind of ota are you? ⮧

—By Tomohiro Machiyama

MANGA

Japanese comics, in case you didn't know. Irresponsible pictures to read, collect, and recycle. Manga are everywhere.

MANDARAKE
See map p. 29

The forces of evil celebrate, as Sailor Saturn sang karaoke rather than save the world.

Sailor Saturn is in the Mandarake store singing anime theme songs. She shares a raised stage with piles of merchandise: toys, model kits, robots, and monsters. Yet no one in the shop pauses to enjoy the pretty Sailor Scout's karaoke concert. Instead, otaku from around the world are too busy hunting and gathering in the alleys of Mandarake shopping for used goods. Some snap up cheap manga or vinyl figures to complete their collections, others gasp in shock at the prices for first editions by *mangaka* (artists) like Osamu Tezuka and Kazuo Umezu. From fine pieces worth tens of thousands of dollars to one-buck figures and comics, all otaku tastes are catered to. Sailor Saturn finishes her karaoke set to no applause and walks back behind the cash register to ring up the next round of customer purchases.

It's October 2002, and I've managed to infiltrate Mandarake's corporate headquarters deep inside the Nakano Broadway shopping complex. I'm seated across from Masuzo Furukawa the founder and CEO of Mandarake, who has this to say about his chain of collector superstores for otaku people:

"Our mission is to take over the world using manga and other otaku things."

Furukawa isn't kidding. The meeting room at Mandarake has been modeled after the HQ of Shocker, the evil organization from the live-action superhero show *Kamen Rider* right down to a set of oval-shaped sliding doors. Behind him is a map of the world, marked by several Mandarake locations in Japan, the US, and Europe. The final inexplicable touch is a nude female mannequin that rests in the corner.

In his early fifties, Furukawa is lean and athletic. His manner is sharp, attentive.

He's overseen his personal empire of manga and anime goods grow from a single antique store twenty-five years ago to an international chain of stores that stock, according to Furukawa's estimation, over one million secondhand items. Currently, there are three Mandarake locations in Tokyo alone: the mother store in Nakano, several decentralized shops in Akihabara, and a big flashy fortress in Shibuya.

Mandarake's CEO Masuzo Furukawa (not to be confused with "Dr. Evil") reveals his plan for world domination.

To walk into any of them is to have the awesome enormity of otaku culture laid out before you: A place where anime, video games, toys, dojinshi (fan-produced manga), and even human beings remade in the form of 2D characters (at the Shibuya store the staff gals dress in cosplay and sing anime theme songs) delight the senses. But don't let the dazzling array of diversity fool you. The foundation of all of it is Japanese comic books. Manga.

* * * * *

Manga first emerged out of Japan's poverty-stricken postwar era and was embraced by a populace hungry for cheap visual entertainment. Creators like Osamu Tezuka and Shotaro Ishinomori created a new style of storytelling based on big eyes and time compressed or stretched out like salt-water taffy. The resulting industry soon made the transition to movies and television in the form of anime. This medium would be the first to bring the manga sensibility to the rest of the world. As Furukawa points out, the word "Mandarake" means "manga is everywhere." A former manga artist himself, he voices a deep respect for what others could consider junk.

"Otaku goods are thought of disposable. The history of these kinds of things is very long, but they are not put in museums. So our job is to keep these items in circulation, like a kind of living archive or library. If no one does this, then a piece of history is gone."

Still, Mandarake is a business, and according to Furukawa, business is good. "Mandarake pulled in $36 million in 2002," he says. "We estimate that we'll be making about $150 million annually within three years."In some ways, Furukawa seems to be running parallel with the modern Japanese manga industry itself. Internationally, manga is as hot as it's ever been. English translations of manga are the fastest–growing segment of the US publishing industry, with annual sales valued around $120 million. Taking over the world seems to be within reach.

If only it were that easy to keep the momentum up back home.

*****

The first time I went to Tokyo in 1999, I expected to see not only giant monsters ransacking skyscrapers but people reading manga, everywhere. Instead, I saw people shunning not just manga, but most forms of print publications. By 2004, the situation had worsened. While advertisements for manga magazines were plentiful on the commuter trains, the number of people actually reading them had dropped to one person per car.

Furukawa mentions that 1996 was the peak year for manga in Japan, when a comic magazine like *Shonen Jump* could have a circulation of six million copies a week—which is how many comic books are sold in the US *annually*.

The drop-off began the next year. Sales for major manga publishers like Shogakukan, Shueisha, and

Kodansha have steadily been going down ever since, to the point where they're half of what they once were.

Simply put, manga just isn't what it used to be, and the reasons are numerous.

Manga scribe Kentaro Takekuma blames the increasing lack of creator-owned properties. Major publishers now develop and license titles like *Yu-gi-oh!* and *Pokémon* themselves, with the resulting cash going directly into company coffers. The majors want blockbusters from creative staff, but artists and writers are paid at shockingly low rates.

Takekuma estimates that the average artist would actually make more money working in a convenience store, while editors and executives help themselves to six-figure salaries. Conditions like these are hardly going to inspire must-read masterpieces.

A complete set of twenty-five early Osamu Tezuka works can be yours now for a mere $12,500.

If you can't spare the big bucks, here're some classic manga for $650 and $500.

Meanwhile, the same preteen boys that most of today's comics are created for have made the switch to portable video game devices. Adults have their own version of the Game Boy, and a whole lot more, in the *keitai*—the cell phone—a technology that's revolutionizing 21st-century Japan while leaving older media behind in the dirt.

The publishing industry is trying to find

ways to deliver manga content directly to cell phones and computer screens. But "digital shoplifting," that is, photographing the pages of books and magazines using a cell-phone camera, have already cut out the middleman.

Tomo's theory is that when the dust finally settles manga will wind up a generational thing like "Classic Rock" here in the States, where a dedicated, never-growing audience demands the same old songs over and over, and where the groupies don't get any younger. If so, this would be bad news not just for manga publishers but for folks like Mandarake's Masuzo Furukawa.

* * * * *

Soon after the interview, Mandarake closes down its Shinjuku branch. The USA store, located in Santa Monica, follows suit. Furukawa has had to start diversifying his product line. As of this writing, there's a sexual harassment case pending against Furukawa, filed by an ex-Mandarake employee. But that hasn't stopped the chain from selling a photo book in which Furukawa ties up female Mandarake employees and shaves their pubic hair. (No secret, as Mandarake's own publicist showed a copy to me, smiling as he flipped through the pages.) And tucked away between the mountains of manga and anime, Mandarake also hawks a line of books and videos espousing Furukawa's New Age beliefs, which sometimes take an alarming turn into doomsday prophecies.

So is this finally it? The end of the world that manga hath wrought?

"Otaku culture is just like any other culture," Furukawa says, "There are two needs: first, the country should be rich, and the second is there needs to be freedom of expression, just like Europe during the Renaissance, and the Impressionist movement in France. You need to be able to make anything you want: even stories involving Lolicon, violence, and sex. That's why Japan has the biggest otaku culture."

Outside the meeting room, several pretty young girls wait patiently to be interviewed for job positions. Looking good helps and knowing about manga is a plus, but that's not all Furukawa needs. As he says, "It took more than ten years to get the employees to simply say hello to the customers because they are not social people. I want them to be more extroverted. Sometimes I try and make small talk, even about otaku kinds of things. But it's hard. They've got a lot of problems." ∋

Never mind the doomsday prophecies, mister manager. Where are the nude photo books of the female employees?

Address: 5-52-15 Nakano, Nakano-ku, Tokyo
Tel: 03-3228-0007
Site: http://www.mandarake.co.jp

Tora no Ana
See map p. 83

A cute little girl stands twenty feet high in the Tokyo skyline. She has the classic big anime eyes, little feline ears, and a striped tail flowing out behind you, just to let you know she's a tiger. Where else but in Akihabara would you see a building like this?

The Akihabara area may look like a happy place full of smiling anime faces and otaku lost in fetish-induced trance states. But underneath the surface is a battle for control of its lucrative manga and dojinshi racket. The area is crowded with retailers selling comics from both major publishers and from the fan press (AKA dojinshi). But only one store gets to be the king of the jungle on both fronts: Tora no Ana. Fittingly, the name means "Tiger Pit," and it is a reference to a training school for wicked pro wrestlers from the classic *Tiger Mask* manga.

A single building isn't enough to contain

According to the sign, there are five kinds of *moe* at Tora no Ana, one per floor presumably!

Tora no Ana. Its Akiba (as the locals call the neighborhood) empire is spread across three separate stores all located within walking distance of each other. Tora no Ana 1 (AKA Comic Tora no Ana) is the flagship store, housed in a colorful skyscraper that dominates Akihabara's main drag of Chuo-dori. The basement is full of "adult goods": dirty comics, DVDs, and PC games. The first floor is a far less shady proposition and is devoted to a big selection of mainstream manga books and magazines of both Shonen (Boys') and Shojo (Girls') varieties. Anime-related goods like CDs, DVDs, figures (some of them life-sized), and trading cards are located on the second level, while dojinshi publications and dojin soft dominate floors three and four.

Tora no Ana 3 is just down the street. It's a used manga and dojinshi emporium with a "buying center" located on the top floor. And if that wasn't enough, tucked away on a side street nearby is Tora no Ana 2, which houses three more levels of mainstream comics, outrageous adult material, and very explicit dojinshi.

There are other Tora no Ana stores in Tokyo, including a new location in Shinjuku and another mammoth shop in Ikebukuro. But the Akihabara locations get full marks for transforming the neighborhood. When you see Tora no Ana 1's building, emblazoned with its trademark cute tiger girl character, gaze upon it mighty and rejoice. You are at the epicenter of the otaku revolution. Who needs the twice annual Comic Market, when you can be supplied with dojinshi all year round? ₴

Address: 4-3-1 Sotokanda, Chiyoda-ku, Tokyo
Tel: 03-5294-0123
Site: http://www.toranoana.co.jp/

Shopping
Prices estimated in US$

Hungry Man
(Aiueo Boy)
Hardboiled manga with the emphasis on "Man."
1978 first edition. Originally sold for $5. Bought at Mandarake for $3.

Sacrifice of the Sex Demon
(Inran no Ikenie)
Volume 3 of Dirty Matsumoto's "Dirty Collection."
1980 first edition. Originally sold for $5. Bought at Mandarake for $4.

Akumetsu Vol. 1
By Yoshiaki Tabata and Yuki Yogo. Jan Kurotaki recommends this boys' comic about political assassinations. Bought new from K Books for $3.90.

Crusher Joe Big Encyclopedia
Anime tie-in edited by Tomo Machiyama! 1983 first edition. Originally sold for $6.50. Bought at Mandarake for $15.

Leiji Matsumoto Big Manga Book
Classic manga super-sized 1979 first edition. Originally sold for $3.80. Bought at Mandarake for $15.

Shopping
Prices estimated in US$

Little Susumu's Big Shock
(Susumu-chan Dai Shock)
Horror short–story collection by Go Nagai. Bought new for $3.33 from 7-Eleven.

Bloody Angel
(Chi Mamire Tenshi)
By Jun Hayami. Erotic-grotesque mayhem. Bought new from Taco ché for $8.50

Fireworks
By Junko Mizuno 1996–2002 short–story collection. Bought new from Kinokuniya Bookstore for $9.99.

Kamen Rider Spirits Vol. 1
By Shotaro Ishinomori and Kenichi Muraeda. Retro superhero action. Bought new from Tora no Ana for $5.50.

Kamen Rider Monster Big Encyclopedia
Rubber monster attack. 1981 first edition. Originally sold for $7.50. Bought at Mandarake for $20.

Taco Ché
See map p. 29

Imagine a store that would sell any kind of manga, no matter how weird or incredibly strange. It's in Tokyo and it's called Taco ché.

In the beginning, there was a fast-food restaurant in the Takadanobaba area specializing in *takoyaki* (fried octopus balls). Eventually the cooks moved out, the kitchen went cold, and a new establishment opened up in the building. They kept half of the store's original name,

"Taco" (spelling it with a "c") and then perversely added the French-sounding word "ché" to the end. Thus was born Taco ché. They've since moved to the Nakano Broadway shopping center, but the house specialty is the same: manga and other media from the cutting edge of the Japanese underground.

Originally operating as the official store of the legendary avant-garde comic magazine *Garo* (where artists like Tsuge Yoshiharu and Hideshi Hino published some of their most revolutionary work in the '60s and '70s), Taco ché's current selection of manga includes mind-bending works by artists like Junko Mizuno (*Pure Trance*) and Suehiro Maruo (*Mr. Arashi's Amazing Freak Show*). Even more far-out mixes of the erotic and grotesque can also be found in the pages of manga by Dirty Matsumoto and Jun Hayami (*Beauty Labyrinth of Razors*), perhaps the most downright disturbing-yet-mesmerizing *mangaka* of all time.

Whatever your tastes (it helps if they are a bit off the beaten path), the accommodating staff, which includes manga author and historian Shohei Onishi, will be happy to assist you in finding an eye-opening alternative to the usual mass-produced fare.

Taco ché also stocks independently produced small press items ranging from elaborate dojinshi to insane, gibbering Xeroxed tracts. You'll also find T-shirts, CDs, videos postcards, and limited-edition photo books featuring simulated acts of *hara-kiri* that will have your Giant Robot magazine–reading friends green with envy.

So if not from major publisher, where does all this crazy stuff come from? Like San Francisco's beatnik mecca City Lights, the door to distribution, if not fame, is wide open. Anyone can bring in an item to Taco ché and sell it on consignment. Nothing, no matter how strange, is refused. As storeowner Ayumi Nakayama says, "We will sell anything here, as long as it is independently produced."

Presumably, even fried octopus balls. ⌑

Address: Nakano Broadway 3F, 5-52-15 Nakano, Nakano-ku, Tokyo
Site: http://www.tacoche.com/

Taco ché mascot Panda Rabu launches a reverse flying elbow drop on store staffers Shohei Onishi (l) and Ayumi Nakayama (r).

GeraGera Manga Cafe
See map p. 141

Rows and rows of huge bookshelves stuffed with manga paperbacks stretch out before me. From just a cursory glance I can see old comic classics like *Lone Wolf and Cub* and *Violence Jack* alongside new stuff like *Naruto* and *One Piece*. It's all mine for the reading, and it will hardly do any damage to my wallet.

It used to be that I'd check my e-mail at a Kinko's copy shop in Shinjuku Ward. The service was fine, but as with most Kinko's there wasn't any incentive to hang out once I'd finished my business.

Eventually, Tomo suggested that I consider switching allegiances. "Stop going to Kinko's!" he yelled. "Go to a Manga Café instead! You can check your e-mail and even get free coffee there! And you can read all the manga you want! It's a paradise for otaku!"

I figured comics and free coffee had to be a better scene than boring old Kinko's, so off I went in search of the nearest manga café.

By some estimates, there are more Internet and manga cafes in Tokyo than there are Starbucks. The leading chain right now is called GeraGera. With locations all over the place, the closest one to the hotel was located smack in the middle of Kabuki-cho, Tokyo's berserk red light district.

I braved a gauntlet of drunks, prostitutes, and a variety of gangsters until I saw the

sign outside. It read: "GeraGera Manga Café. 40,000 comics to choose from. 200 video games. Computers with high-speed data connections. DVDs. CDs. TVs. Massage chairs. Free coffee."

With 40,000 manga to choose from, what more do you want? Idol photo books? GeraGera's got them too (l).

The streets may have been crawling with scum and villainy, but the interior of GeraGera was immaculate and clean. You get one hour of access to the attraction of your choice for around 4 bucks US. You even can do a hit-and-run ten-minute session for about 50 cents, which makes it a much better deal than Kinko's if you just want to check your email. And for the heavy user, or for folks who missed the last train home, there's what they call "The Night Pack." Throw down 13 bucks and you can camp out at GeraGera from 11:30 p.m. to 6 a.m. But inevitably, no matter what time you wander in, you'll see as many people passed out in their cozy computer pens as you will see reading manga.

GeraGera cafes are popping up all over Tokyo, and I've counted three locations in

the Shinjuku area alone (the Kabuki-cho one wins for size and English-friendly staff). All are hated by the manga publishing industry, who estimate that a single graphic novel is read by as many as 100 people. All the money goes directly to the café owners, who don't believe in paying royalties.

I'd start playing the violin over these lost profits, but I've got to save my last ounce of sympathy for Kinko's. ⮠

Address: Humax Pavilion 2F, 1-20-1 Kabuki-cho, Shinjuku-ku, Tokyo
Tel: 03-5285-0585
Site: http://www.geragera.co.jp/indexN.html

The Cheapest Manga in Tokyo

You'll see them around every major train station or sitting on the sidewalk at busy thoroughfares: old men (a fair share of them homeless) hawking the latest manga books and magazines, at a mere fraction of the cover price.

The convenience stores and secondhand shops like Book Off may be selling massive "My First Wide" editions of Rumiko Takahashi's *Maison Ikkoku* for fewer than 5 bucks. But if you choose to buy it off the street, you can expect to pay about half of that. Even better, unlike the usual "no haggling" policy that usually goes hand in hand with shopping in Tokyo, these guys are actually willing to negotiate with you for an even bigger score (for instance, maybe you're not going to eat the rest of that hamburger?).

What's the secret of their outrageously low, low prices? Let's just say that the manga for sale are used. Like, real used. Picked up from the overhead bins on the trains, or fished out from the trash mostly. But best not to think about that too much.

Instead, behold the very bottom of the manga food chain. After this, Japan's famed comic books become toilet paper, and then are recycled, only to become manga once more. ↻

MAP

The otaku mega mall. Minutes from Nakano Station. Home to Mandarake and specialty shops for maniacs. Also includes clothing for little old ladies, tasty restaurants, chiropractors, and crystal-wielding psychics. A madder building is hard to imagine.

2F

NAKANO BROADWAY

Torio
03-5343-2333
Secondhand publications on idols, j-pop, subculture, music, & movies.

Alf
03-3389-7156
Store for collectors of "Choro Q" toy cars. Also carries food goods.

Doraku
03-3228-3534
Collector's shop for movie maniacs. Posters, pamphlets, stills, & fliers.

Mandarake Gallery
Original art, autographs, & posters from famous manga artists.

Rough.
03-5318-2271
http://www.toyshop-rough.com/
Specializing in Hong Kong imports & stylish Japanese figures such as Kubrick.

Toy's Air Mail
03-5913-6277
Exclusive store for Hong Kong figure maker Hot Toys and a specialty shop store for 12" action figures.

Commit
03-3389-8809
http://www.anime-commit.com/
Original animation cells.

TO WAVE
03-3389-5657
Rental Showcase.

VENTVERT
03-3388-0631
http://www.vent-vert.com/
Featuring rare & premium Hello Kitty & San Rio merchandise.

Merry-go-Round Collector's Toy Store
03-3319-7900
Featuring Bandai toys from around the world. Also specializing in Tomy, Yujin, & Medicom brands.

Idol Shop Utahime Domu
03-3387-9230
Idol CD shop.

Mandarake Gachaten
Gachapon, trading cards, & custom goods.

Mandarake Daisharin
Store for toy & model vehicles from makers like Tamiya & Corgi.

Mandarake Galaxy
Vintage video game hardware & software. Famicom, Game Boy, Sega Saturn, Dreamcast, Playstation, 3DO.

Mandarake Live
New & used women's dojinshi store. Spotlight on works by the staff.

Mandarake Micro
Small toys.

Mandarake Deep
Dojinshi store for men.

Mandarake Special 2
CD, Video, LD, DVD, & even some Gachapon.

Mandarake Special 1
Vintage Japanese toys & model kits. Die-cast metal, vinyl figures, and garage kits.

Map

coffee shop
TORIO
commercial district office
BROADWAY TOURIST
coffee shop EMU
ALF
TORIO 2
PHONE
ELEVATOR
ESCALATOR
UTAHIME DOMU
KO RINBO
SUZU KOBO
BELL FRIEND
BATHROOM
haircut ROSHERU
cafe HORUN
jewel UNO
udon & soba RYOGOKU
LOTUS
kimono JINEMON
DISC FIVE
chiropractor SAKURA
SAKURA ART GALLERY
movie posters DORAKU
outlet WHITE PINE
NARUKIYA HERUGA
coin-op massage chair KUTSUROGI SHITEISEKI
haircut FRANCE
ELEVATOR STREET
SAKAKOSHI COFFEE SHOP
MANDARAKE GALLERY
ART SHISHU
CENTURY 21
NARUKIYA HERUGA
MATSUE SUSHI
NARUKIYA HERUGA
cell phone-PAO
FURIMARU.COM
AWS WONDER BROADWAY
STAIRS
FIFTY FIFTY
ANIDOSU
select toy shop ROUGH.
MANDARAKE GACHATEN
PHONE
MANDARAKE DAISHARIN
ROUGH
NOZAKI COIN
haircut SUPARU
antique AJISAI
ELEVATOR
STAIRS
food NEGIBOZU
TOY'S AIR MAIL
TOY'S AIR MAIL
woman's dojinshi MANDARAKE LIVE
MANDARAKE GALAXY
haircut SUDOU
food MARIKOTEI
tonkatsu rest. KOIKE
audio & electronics shop KAGOYA
SAITO ACCOUNTANT OFFICE
COLLECTION BOX+KEY
COLLECTOR'S ALLEY
okonomiyaki rest. HIMAWARI
men's dojinshi MANDARAKE DEEP
secondhand shop ASAMI
MANDARAKE MICRO
cell COMMIT
MANDARAKE SPECIAL 2
haircut CHIGUSA
boutique 219
women's clothing MIMURA
rental showcase-TO WAVE
STAIRS
sanrio shop VENTVERT
VENTVERT
PHONE
accessories MIMURA
niigata food YUKI TSUBAKI
toy store MERRY-GO-ROUND
MANDARAKE SPECIAL 1
food KAGARI
BATHROOM
STAIRS
BROADWAY STREET

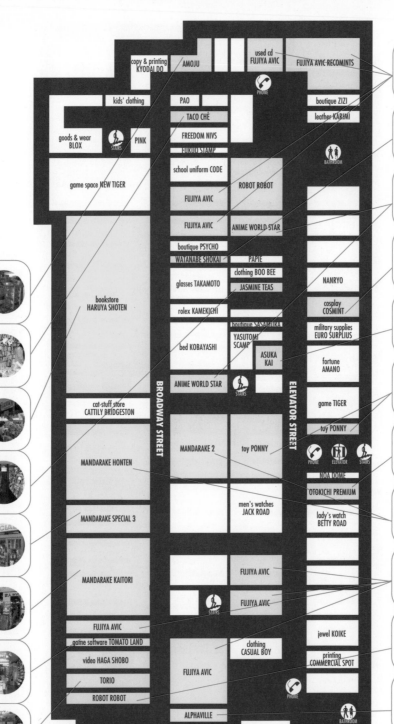

Map labels:

copy & printing KYODAI DO · AMOJU · used cd FUJIYA AVIC · FUJIYA AVIC-RECOMINTS
PHONE
kids' clothing · PAO · boutique ZIZI
TACO CHÉ · leather KARIMI
goods & wear BLOX · STAIRS · PINK · FREEDOM NIVS · FUKUO STAMP
BATHROOM
game space NEW TIGER · school uniform CODE · ROBOT ROBOT
FUJIYA AVIC
FUJIYA AVIC · ANIME WORLD STAR
boutique PSYCHO
WATANABE SHOKAI · PAPIE · NANRYO
bookstore HARUYA SHOTEN · glasses TAKAMOTO · clothing BOO BEE
JASMINE TEAS · cosplay COSMINT
rolex KAMEKICHI · boutique SASAMURA
bed KOBAYASHI · YASUTOMI SCAMP · military supplies EURO SURPLIUS
ASUKA KAI · fortune AMANO
ANIME WORLD STAR · STAIRS · game TIGER
BROADWAY STREET · ELEVATOR STREET · toy PONNY
cat-stuff store CATTILY BRIDGESTON
MANDARAKE 2 · toy PONNY · PHONE ELEVATOR STAIRS
MANDARAKE HONTEN · NOA DOME
OTOKICHI PREMIUM
MANDARAKE SPECIAL 3 · men's watches JACK ROAD · lady's watch BETTY ROAD
MANDARAKE KAITORI · FUJIYA AVIC
FUJIYA AVIC · STAIRS · FUJIYA AVIC
FUJIYA AVIC · jewel KOIKE
game software TOMATO LAND · clothing CASUAL BOY · printing COMMERCIAL SPOT
video HAGA SHOBO
TORIO · FUJIYA AVIC
ROBOT ROBOT · PHONE
ALPHAVILLE · BATHROOM
STAIRS

Left column directory:

Amoju
03-5318-0401
http://www.amoju.com/frame.htm
Collector's toy store.

Taco Ché
03-5343-3010
http://www.tacoche.com/
Indie media & comics.

Haruya Shoten
03-3387-8451
Bookstore.

Jasmine Teas
03-5345-7023
CDs from China & Singapore.

Mandarake Special 3
New toys.

Mandarake Kaitori
Used goods buyback.

Tomato Land
03-3387-8388
Video games & software.

Torio
03-5343-2333
Used magazines & books about idols, j-pop, subculture, music, & movies. Also sells movie memorabilia & promo goods.

Right column directory:

Fujiya Avic
03-3386-5917
http://www.fujiya-avic.co.jp/
Used audio/video & software.

Watanabe Shokai
03-3387-6855
Knives, model guns, air guns, and wooden swords.

Anime World Star
03-3386-0389
http://www.anime-world-star.com/alfa/
Animation cells store.

Cosmint
03-5345-5315
http://www.cosmint.co.jp/
Cosplay store.

Asuka Kai
03-3228-3777
Psychic & fortune-telling store.

Ponny
03-3387-7451
Fancy & cute goods store.

Otokichi Premium
03-3389-6628
http://www.otokichi.com/main/newotokichien/engtop.htm
Used '60s–'70s CDs, LPs, & rare videos.

Mandarake
03-3385-6459
http://www.mandarake.co.jp/
The original Mandarake manga store. See p.18.

Fujiya Avic
03-3386-5917
http://www.fujiya-avic.co.jp/
Used audio/video software.

Robot Robot
03-5345-7553
http://www.robotrobot.com/catalog/
Playmobil, PEZ, action figures, Snoopy, Smurfs, soft vinyl, Gachapon, & Choco Eggs.

Alphaville
03-3387-0123
Hard to find PC software & games.

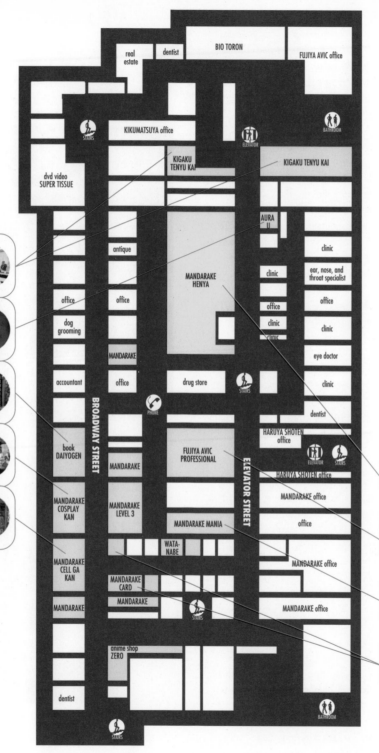

Kigaku Tenyu Kai
03-3228-0341
Fortune-telling
lectures.

Aura U
03-3228-4425
Aura-capturing photo
service.

Daiyogen
03-3387-5707
http://www.toky-
obbs.or.jp/daiyogen/
New Age & cult book-
store.

**Mandarake
Cosplay Kan**
Used cosplay outfits
& accessories.

**Mandarake Cell Ga
Kan**
Original animation
cells including items
from Studio Ghibli,
*Lupin III, Gundam,
Evangelion,* etc.

Mandarake Henya
Rare collector's items
from the Showa era.

Fujiya Avic Professional
03-3386-5910
http://www.fujiya-
avic.co.jp/
Used audio/video
equipment for profes-
sionals.

**Mandarake
Mania**
Vintage comics &
anime magazines.

Mandarake Card
Trading cards of
idols, sports, and
monsters.

Map labels:
- real estate
- dentist
- BIO TORON
- FUJIYA AVIC office
- STAIRS
- KIKUMATSUYA office
- ELEVATOR
- BATHROOM
- dvd video SUPER TISSUE
- KIGAKU TENYU KAI
- KIGAKU TENYU KAI
- AURA U
- clinic
- ear, nose, and throat specialist
- antique
- clinic
- office
- office
- MANDARAKE HENYA
- office
- clinic
- dog grooming
- clinic
- clinic
- eye doctor
- MANDARAKE
- accountant
- office
- drug store
- STAIRS
- clinic
- PHONE
- dentist
- HARUYA SHOTEN office
- book DAIYOGEN
- BROADWAY STREET
- FUJIYA AVIC PROFESSIONAL
- ELEVATOR
- STAIRS
- MANDARAKE
- HARUYA SHOTEN office
- MANDARAKE COSPLAY KAN
- MANDARAKE LEVEL 3
- ELEVATOR STREET
- MANDARAKE office
- MANDARAKE MANIA
- office
- MANDARAKE CELL GA KAN
- WATA-NABE
- MANDARAKE office
- MANDARAKE CARD
- MANDARAKE
- MANDARAKE office
- STAIRS
- anime shop ZERO
- dentist
- BATHROOM
- STAIRS

The old man in the tobacco shop window looks like a wax statute that's been there since 1954. Posters for old Showa-era idol movies are displayed in store windows. Inside are bins of old-fashioned candy and junk food, along with 45rpm records.

There's the heavenly scent of slightly burnt soy sauce hanging in the air. Hidden speakers play old pop hits from decades past. Over at the arcade, a little kid puts down his Game Boy long enough to shoot at targets with a cork gun. A group of young Japanese women try out American pinball, probably for the first time. Ancient Panasonic television sets broadcast old black-and-white episodes of *Astro Boy*.

Is this really Odaiba, the city of the future? Heck, what year is it?

Maybe you'd like to go to Japan to see an inspiring vision of tomorrow: trains propelled by magnetic levitation, humanoid robots made by Sony, cell phones smarter than most human beings—that sort of thing.

But when I go to Tokyo, it's to search for signs of the past. I spend the days digging for vintage clothes, LPs, and old anime, manga, and toys. Why? Because in my humble opinion, the late Showa era was when otaku culture and Japan was at its peak. If time had stopped somewhere between 1954 and 1989, that would be fine with me.

I'm not the only one who feels this way. Japan is in the grips of a Natsukashi ("nostalgia") Boom. It first began in the mid-'80s when academics started searching for hidden meanings in the anime and manga of their childhood. After the Bubble Economy started to pop in 1989, a long recession settled in, and the warm glow of the "good old days" beckoned to the masses. Since then, only technology has progressed. Pop culture has

(Clockwise from right) A *Showa Diorama Figure* depicting an old-time storyteller, the general store inside the Odaiba Natsukashi Mall, a tobacco vendor at the Natsukashi Mall, 1958 eternal at the Shin Yokohama Ramen Museum.

gone in the opposite direction.

Anime and manga are now overpopulated with remakes and rereleases. Advertising agencies routinely trot out old characters like Astro Boy and Joe Yabuki (from *Tomorrow's Joe*) to help rope in middle-aged consumers. Television is clogged with retrospectives and clip shows highlighting yesterday's celebrities.

The past is reclaiming the present on all fronts. The landfill town of Odaiba is supposed to be the ultra-modern "city of tomorrow." But it is also home to a "Natsukashi Mall," which tries to evoke the feel of postwar Japan through rickety food stands, tobacco shops, candy vendors, and general stores filled with replicas of old products (too bad the illusion falls apart once you see the price tags).

At the Ramen Museum in Shin (New) Yokohama, you'll find "Ramen Town," a painstaking re-creation of a Tokyo cityscape circa 1958. From concealed speakers in fabricated back alleys come the taped sounds of strolling singers and bar fights. You can peep in on a typical postwar Japanese household and watch a black-and-white wrestling match on the TV over and over again as it plays on a loop. There's even a mock-up movie theater, and the show is always the same.

Natsukashi Boom

But the ultimate symbol of the Natsukashi Boom may be the recent PlayStation2 game Bokan: Shonen Club Gaho (Adventure: Boys Club Visual Graffiti) where players assume the role of a young boy who lives in an impossible amalgam of the Showa era, collecting candy, watching TV, and reading manga.

Wouldn't it be more practical for someone to simply try and build a time machine? Heck, I'd pay top dollar to take a spin back to 1967. After all this simulation, I figure I'm ready for the real thing. ⮌

Tiny figures, candy prizes, and dolls for children and adults. Collect them all, or die trying.

TOYS

INTERVIEW WITH THE FIGURE KING

In the palm of my hand is a tiny version of the famed Chestburster from the movie *Alien*. He may have grossed out moviegoers back in 1979, but now as a candy figure from Japan, a kind of glorified Cracker Jack prize, the little guy is cute in his own special way.

Hunting him down was tough. First, I had to drop money on numerous *Alien* candy toys at the convenience store only to find disappointment when I kept getting the much lamer Dog Alien from *Alien 3*. What the heck would it take to complete my collection of *Alien* candy toys from Konami?

When I was just a brat in short pants, my dad gave me a die-cast metal Godzilla monster that he'd picked up on a whim at Japantown in San Francisco. Since then, I've been following the demon's road of Japanese toys and pop culture trinkets at home and abroad.

In 2003, I began contributing a column to the Japanese magazine *Figure Oh* (*Figure King*), the CNN of toys and collectible otaku culture. The readers wanted to know how Japanese toys had invaded the US, so I tried my best to tell them. Meanwhile, for my own sake, I wanted to find out how Japanese toys for me had made the jump from kid stuff to lifelong habit.

While in Tokyo, I got to meet *Figure Oh*'s founding editor, Hisanori Nukata. A maverick in the publishing world, Nukata is a collector himself; a selection of his goods from Hayao Miyazaki's series *Heidi of the Alps* has been displayed in several museums. He's also a living encyclopedia of information about Japanese toys. Over afternoon tea on a rainy fall day in Kabuki-cho, Nukata the Figure King revealed how Japanese figures had recently transformed the collecting habits of the realm.

*****

In the beginning, action figures occupied the same place in Japanese society that they did everywhere else: they were meant for children, and only children, to play with.

But as any kid who grew up coveting *Shogun Warriors* and *Transformers* can tell you, Japanese toys from the '60s onward were truly amazing things to behold. Some of these grown-up kids refused to put away their childish things. Instead, they hunted down old Godzilla vinyl figures made by Marusan and made lists of all known variations in the Chogokin die-cast metal robot toys from Popy. In the '80s, some even made their own figures of favorite characters in the form of elaborate models known as "garage kits," often as colossal in size as they were expensive. Meanwhile, normal folk just viewed this group of adult toy enthusiasts as being a bit weird, AKA "otaku."

Nukata credits the hugely popular TV program, *Kaiun Nandemo Kanteidan* (inspired by the BBC's *Antiques Roadshow*) for getting regular people interested in collecting. Suddenly, otaku-like hoarding started to look downright respectable to the public. After all, some of that old junk was worth big money, and it sure made you feel warm and nostalgic to see those old heroes and villains again.

A year later, Bandai, the leading Japanese toy company, introduced its first capsule toys called "Gashapon," a variation on the generic toy term "Gachapon" (see pp. 42–44). Sold from vending machines, Bandai's "High Grade Series" offered minia-turized *Ultraman* and *Evangelion* goods. For a mere ¥200 (around $2), you could own a 1.5"-high figure with all the detail of a $100 garage kit at a size perfect for a Japanese room or apartment where space was at a premium. Even better, Gachapon were readymade and required no fumbling about with a paintbrush or an Exacto knife.

The craze began first in Akihabara, where Gachapon machines swept up the remaining pocket money of otaku who'd come to "Electric Town" to buy computer parts and games. Quickly, the rest of the populace began to take a liking to these small figures as well, especially middle-aged men roped in by characters from their youth (Nukata believes it was a Bandai executive in his forties named Mistuharu Saito who consistently pushed for nostalgic properties).

Less than a year after the debut of the High Grade Series, Bandai was raking in millions. Their Gachapon were the biggest financial success in the history of Japanese toys. To keep up with demand, Bandai opened a new factory deep in the mountains of China, where employees (hired for their skills at creating folk art souvenirs like drawing pictures on grains of rice) were amazed not by the playthings they had to produce and paint but by new-to-them novelties like electric light and running water.

By circumventing toy stores and retailers, and by offering high-quality goods at such low prices, Bandai had opened a Pandora's box in the form of a little plastic capsule. The rest of the toy industry collectively screamed,"*Yabai!*" ("Its dangerous!") and wondered how to get a piece of the action for themselves.

* * * * *

One of the companies feeling the post-Gachapon pinch was Kaiyodo, which originally specialized in garage kits renowned for their fetishistic detail. An independent outfit with many otaku on staff, Kaiyodo had avoided getting involved with capsule toys for fear of being swallowed up by Bandai. They viewed their garage kits as unique works of art, whereas Bandai was taking a Henry Ford–like approach to mass production. While Kaiyodo's most popular artists toiled on ferocious dinosaurs and giant monsters, a sculptor named Shinobu Matsumura whined that he wanted to make cute little animals instead, a sentiment that earned him the scorn of his peers.

In 1999 Kaiyodo was asked to make small toys for candy company Furuta Seika. Years earlier, Furuta had teamed up with Italian chocolate maker Ferrero to produce "Choco Eggs" to sell in Japan. But sales of these Easter egg–like confectioneries, with toy prizes (AKA omake) instead of yolks, had been sluggish. Even so, Furuta wanted to give Choco Eggs a second chance. Seeking to avoid the hassle of licensing popular characters (Bandai owned the best ones by now, anyway), Furuta asked Kaiyodo to produce small animal figurines—which would be copyright free—for a new line of Choco Eggs.

Shinobu Matsumura stepped up to the plate. He began sculpting animals that were 75 percent anatomically accurate. The remaining 25 percent was filled in by an X-factor called the "kawaii touch," or "cute touch."

Matsumura's animal figures struck gold with a previously untapped market. The result was another revolution. Females, from schoolgirls to office ladies, began collecting omake. Classified as food, not as toys, Choco Eggs immediately had massive distribution through Japan's groceries and convenience stores, which far outnumber toy stores. Sales jumped to 6 million units within months.

A single Choco Egg was the product of three separate nations: China, where the toys were manufactured; Italy, where the chocolate is made; and Japan, where the whole business began. The complex logistics of coordination meant that demand could not be met for some time.

Other toy companies and sweet makers began to form alliances. By 2001, Nukata estimates that over a hundred different companies were offering various forms of candy toys, called shokugan (from shoku, meaning "food," and gan from the Japanese word for "toy," gangu).

But creating a hit candy toy now is seldom a sure thing. Obscure characters, like '70s superhero Denjin Zaboga, can meet modest success thanks to obsessive collectors. Meanwhile, a property like Dragon Ball Z (a juggernaut in media like anime and manga) can mysteriously turn out to be a bust, as the Konami Company found out when it made 100,000 figures that nobody wanted to buy.

Indeed, gambling is key to the candy-toy phenomenon. Like baseball cards, manufacturers often control the rarity of a toy prize, leading to mad demand. A limited-edition figure can go for thousands of dollars on Internet auctions. Then there are those who gamble with their health. Nukata mentions reports of people coming down with diabetes from candy-toy addictions.

Today, candy toys pull in about $500 million annually and are holding steady. Downsizing for both Gachapon and candy toys is inevitable, Nukata says. But the impact they've had will be a lasting one.

And even if candy toys do eventually lose favor, there're plenty of other collectibles waiting to take their place. Already, CD singles of Showa-era hit songs and anime themes are being given away as prizes along with tiny packets of candy. Bandai is even planning to market miniature DVDs of vintage *Ultraman* episodes at convenience stores in this same manner.

So long as such goods can be bought at the corner store or from a vending machine, the date on the package of candy matters little. The socially approved expiration for childish things has been extended indefinitely.

Which is good news for me and my quest for *Alien* figures.

Like Harry Dean Stanton in the movie, I stalk the Chestburster down the dark corridors of Akihabara. When I finally spot him hiding out in a collectors' shop at the Radio Building, he goes for five times what he'd cost if I'd caught him at the convenience store. But at least no one laughed at me when I did my little fist-pump and victory dance. ≥

Shopping

Prices estimated in US$

Nostalgic Heroes and Heroines Hit Collection 2
Candy plus mini (8cm) CD single of *Babel II* theme song. From Bandai. $3 at convenience store.

Godzilla, Mothra, Mecha-Godzilla: Tokyo SOS
Candy plus "*Making Of*" DVD. From Bandai. $4.80 at convenience store.

Showa '50s Nostalgic School Memories Series
Candy plus miniature school crossing play set. From Mega House. $2.50 at convenience store.

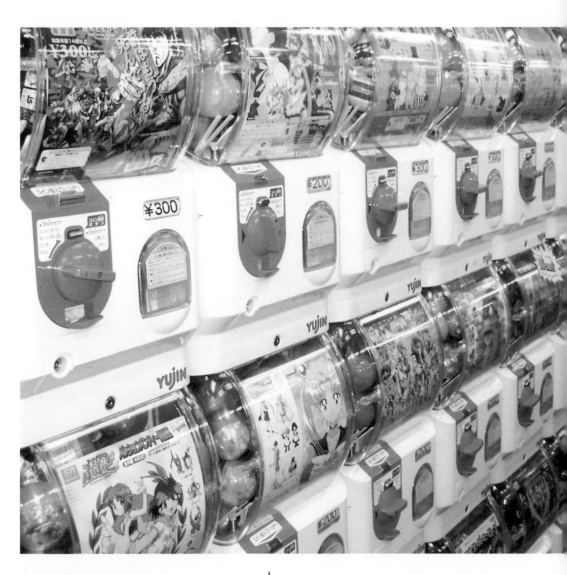

Gachapon
Capsule toys

If Japanese toys are normally like pure unrefined coca leaves, then Gachapon are crack: a cheap, addictive high bound to lead you to ruin.

Imagine those bubblegum or sticker

to thimble-sized replicas of instant ramen.

These capsules are called "Gachapon," a name that comes from the noise the machine makes when the dial is cranked (*gacha*) and the capsule drops (*pon*).

Every Gachapon machine offers something new and different—*Ultraman* monsters, mecha from *Evangelion*, gals from *Sailor Moon*. But lady luck alone determines exactly which capsule toy you'll wind up with. Like the slots in Vegas, you'll probably stand in front of the Gachapon machine for some time throwing away ¥100 coins (each worth about $1) hoping for the elusive jackpot.

I learned the hard way when I tried to score a figure of ape-faced villain Dr. Gori from the '70s superhero show *Spectreman*. Instead I got the extremely lame giant termite monster Bakulah. Not once, but twice in a row.

No wonder people spend big bucks on Gachapon machines. Some accounts place annual returns at around ¥31 billion ($310 million), which means that straight folks and otaku alike are in the grips of capsule toy addiction.

Gachapon machines show up frequently wherever anime, manga, and games are. Naturally, the otaku town of Akihabara is a breeding ground for capsule toys. If you want to hit as many different machines as possible at once, head for the establishment called "Akihabara Gachapon Kaikan" located on an Akiba

vending machines you've seen at the supermarket ever since you were a grubby little kid. Now imagine them filled with plastic capsules containing brilliantly detailed toys and figures ranging from your favorite anime and game characters side street.

Inside this warehouse-like space, you'll find 350 different capsule toy machines all lined up and ready for the picking. Bill changers stand by to transform your paper money into coins, trashcans are overflowing with empty capsules but can handle a few more, and the staff doesn't care how long you hang so long as you keep the machines busy.

But before you give up hope on winning the toy you actually want, there're plenty of shops in Akihabara where you can walk right in and buy it. Conveniently, such a store is located just upstairs from Gachapon Kaikan. That's how I wound up finally scoring my Dr. Gori figure. Sure it cost me three times what it would have if I'd won him fair and square, but at least now I can sleep at night. ₴

Address: MN Building 1F, 3-15-5 Sotokanda, Chiyoda-ku, Tokyo
Tel: 03-5209-6020
Site: http://www.geestore.com/real_gee/mn/

Shopping
Prices estimated in US$

Alien Candy Toys Assortment
Everything but the Chestburster. $27.50 from various convenience stores.

Gamera Vs. Viras Figure Set
In loving memory of the 1968 classic film. $4 from Figure Shop Mint in Akihabara.

X Seijin Gachapon Figure
Godzilla HG Series 7. $6 from Liberty 7 in Akihabara.

Dr. Gori Gachapon Figure
Evil genius space ape from *Spectreman* TV show. $5 from Liberty 7 in Akihabara.

Creature From the Black Lagoon Candy Toy
Part of the Universal Studios Monsters series. $3.60 from Yellow Submarine G-Shop 2 in Akihabara.

Bandai Museum

A giant Gundam robot turns its massive head to gaze at the puny humans who have been lifted up in a hydraulically operated crane. A young father stands next to his child on the raised platform. Dad is wearing the uniform of a Federation officer. Junior is clad in a red jump suit that makes him a soldier of the Principality of Zion—the enemy. While the little guy looks up cautiously at the big guy, Dad cracks a grin a mile wide. He's having more fun at the Bandai Museum than his kid is.

In the 1980s, the Bandai company demolished its competition in the Japanese toy biz by learning to cater not just to children but to adult toy collectors as well. Now, despite recently posting its first-ever net losses, Bandai is Japan's biggest toy conglomerate and an all-around media giant to boot.

Success deserves a monument to

itself, and the Bandai Museum, which opened in the summer of 2003 and occupies six floors of an eight-story building in the working-class suburb of Matsuo, is it.

Don't expect to find bronze busts of legendary shareholders inside, or a corporate history of how Bandai clawed its way to the top, let alone a moving tribute to the folks in China who actually make most of today's "Japanese" toys.

The Bandai Museum was designed as a modern family attraction and is eager to please as many demographics as it can (heck, there's even a pachinko parlor on the first floor). And unlike the designated nerd-only zones of Akihabara and Nakano Broadway, actual normal people can be found inside, along with packs of little kids in short pants who've come to meet

guns and helmets from the One-Year War, slated to begin in Universal Century 0079.

The Wonder Town area offers some of that "good-old fashioned" nostalgia via a shooting gallery, a dime shop, and vintage toys and games that beckon from behind frosted glass. There's also Character World: a walk-through tour that overcomes numerous licensing nightmares to showcase the anime and live-action worlds of *Mazinger Z*, *Ultraman*, *Godzilla*, *Go Ranger* (the original *Power Rangers*), along with a section dedicated to anime

costumed heroes, such as Kamen Rider, when they perform in elaborate stage shows.

You might expect a hyperactive childlike energy to course throughout the building. Instead, the atmosphere is exceedingly calm and relaxed. Drifting around the Bandai Museum aimlessly on a Sunday proved to be the perfect hangover cure for me after a wild night of carousing and karaoke.

Highlights of the venue include a self-contained Gundam Museum, which contains elaborate fake relics such as laser

(From top left) Super Robot toys on display, Kamen Rider V3 says "peace, brother" (r), and a little kid considers joining the Go Ranger task force (bottom).

heroines. With rare toys lined up behind exhibit cases, flanked by Madame Tussauds–styled statues of heroes to marvel at, it makes for the real heart and soul of the Bandai Museum.

Admission to the individual attractions is cheap. Around ¥300 each. But you are strongly encouraged to spend one way or another, whether at restaurants or gift shops. Serious collectors like myself, who practically built the museum via their hopeless addictions, probably own much of the permanent collection anyway and can spiral further into debt at Um's Shop, located on the third floor, which specializes in limited-edition T-shirts and goods.

But the must-see centerpiece of the Bandai Museum is a 1/1 scale (that's life size, for those of you who never made plastic model kits) replica bust of the famed RX-78-2 Mobile Suit from the original *Gundam* series. Standing about twenty feet high and occupying two whole floors, it is all but impossible to miss. For a few extra yen, the helpful staff will

suit you up in either a Federation or Zion uniform (the chocolate and vanilla of the *Gundam* universe) and hoist you up in a crane for the photo opportunity of a lifetime. Across the way in the chic Gundam Café, total strangers will coolly assess your geek-out freak-out while they munch on overpriced curries and spaghetti. ⮐

Address: Piaza Matsudo Building, 1230-1 Matsudo, Matsudo-shi, Chiba-ken
Tel: 047-331-7501
Site: http://www.bandai-museum.jp/english/main.html

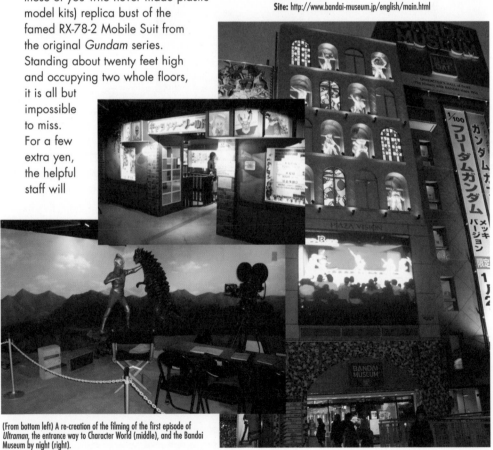

(From bottom left) A re-creation of the filming of the first episode of *Ultraman*, the entrance way to Character World (middle), and the Bandai Museum by night (right).

Dollers

It is said that Hayao Miyazaki's 1979 film *Lupin III: Castle of Cagliostro* brought the Lolita Complex into anime when its two middle-aged protagonists, Lupin and Cagliostro, fought over the affections of a teenage girl named Clarisse. What has in Japan become known as the "Lolicon" sensibility already had a long literary tradition in the West, where it was associated with intellectual decadents like Lewis Carroll and Nabokov.

Recently however, you can hear otaku saying, "Lolicon is old school! Doll Love is going to be in from now on!" The leader of this Doll Love movement is Mamoru Oshii, an internationally acclaimed anime director whom Japan points to with as much pride as it does Miyazaki. When Oshii was asked to make his 2004 film *Ghost in the Shell 2: Innocence*, he put his taste for Surrealist photographer Hans Bellmer's life-sized dolls into the work. *Innocence*'s story—about female sex androids that kill their owners—is possible only in a Lolicon country like Japan. The androids are modeled after little girls, similar to the Bellmer dolls. Oshii, however, repeatedly insists in his film that an android is not simply a substitute for a real girl, but that a doll itself *IS* the ideal girl. As he has said, "Dolls don't have an ugly thing called a heart [he means "ego"] so a doll is beautiful and perfect." Oshii is not alone in his outlandish

sentiments. So-called Dollers, or doll collectors, are already becoming a large segment of the otaku world.

The source of the doll boom may have been the life-size figures of Rei Ayanami, the heroine of *Neon Genesis Evangelion*, that the Paper Moon Company put on the market in March 1996. These dolls cost more than $5,000 each and were produced in a limited edition of thirty. But they were immediately sold out through reservations and high demand.

Paper Moon then began selling life-size dolls of other Bishojo characters like Asuka from *Evangelion*, Card Captor Sakura, and characters from the Gal game *Tokimeki Memorial*. Released one after another, they ranged in price from $2,500 to $5,000 but sold well. The most common rationalization to purchase the doll was: "I could own the sort of girl I saw on the monitor but could never have for real."

Paper Moon also began selling original life-size dolls as part of its "Caramel Ribbon" line; these dolls were not modeled on specific characters but had unique and original anime-styled faces. This might prove that "anime aesthetics" in Japan have already become independent of animation itself. The typical doll owner enjoys naming his doll and goes as far as assigning the doll exactly the personality and character he desires.

The Dolfie doll series, made by the Volks Company, is an "assemble it yourself" kit. Dolfie dolls are meticulously detailed, even more so than European antique-style dolls. They come in the 27-cm-tall Standard doll or the 57-cm Super Dolfie. The line''s biggest sales feature is its "Full Choice System." You can choose from 30 different kinds of heads, 22 kinds of eyeballs, and 186 kinds of wigs, along with all sorts of other body parts to create a totally unique doll. Expect to pay about $750 total for a complete Super Dolfie.

There are not only beautiful-girl dolls, but also pretty-boy dolls whose collectors include men and women of all ages. Collectors hold "Dolpa," doll parties, to show off or sell original costumes for their dolls.

The fun of having a doll is not just dressing it up, but cuddling with it. Some users say that Paper Moon's life-size dolls are too hard owing to their FRP (Fiber Reinforced Plastic) bodies. Others complain that Dolfies are too small and fragile. The Fantastic Soft Figures line is the solution. These are Love Dolls, or so-called sex dolls, with an anime face; they are made by the company Orient Industry, which sells them under the brand name Fantastics. Their selling point is their soft skin and, of course, their functional genitalia.

Users love the doll not as a substitute for a human girlfriend or an anime character. They affectionately call their dolls *musume* ("daughter") and consider the purchase of one as *omukae* ("adoption"). Some spend most of their income on doll clothes and roll them around in wheelchairs for dates. It's better than a real woman because you can own as many mistresses as you want with no sneaking around. There's no cost for food, and best of all they don't talk back.

But from what I've heard, the biggest problem with dolls is that you can't get rid of them because the emotional attachment to them becomes overwhelming. Many Dollers live with a dozen or so life-size dolls in their small apartments. What would they do if there was a fire? ⇄

—By Tomohiro Machiyama

Papermoon official site: http://www.secure.pmoon.co.jp

Volks Dolfie official site (English): http://www.volks.co.jp/en/
Volks Showroom: Radio Kaikan 6F (at the South Exit of Akihabara Station)
Tel: 03-5295-8160

Fantastics official site: http://www.fanta-room.com/

Orient Industry showroom: Suguru Bldg. 2F, 5-23-11 Ueno, Taito-ku, Tokyo
Tel: 03-3832-4832

Mondo Tokyo:
MOE

"Moeeeeeeeeh!"

The word most frequently cried out by the crowds in Akihabara or at Comiket has got to be *moe* (pronounced "mo-eh"). And *moe* might be the single most important keyword to understanding otaku in Japan today.

There are various opinions as to how otaku came to use *moe* for expressing their enchantment with so-called Lolicon (Lolita Complex) characters. Maybe it is a shortened version of Tomoe, which is Sailor Saturn's real name in *Sailor Moon*. Others say it's from Moe Sagisawa from the 1993 anime TV series *Kyoryu Wakusei (Dinosaur Planet)*, and some say it originated from the Japanese word *moeru*, which means "burning" and describes fans' passion toward animation characters (even though a different Chinese character is used).

Fundamentally, *moe* is a verb that means "a plant sprouting." This wholesome image is sometimes used as a metaphor for budding love, as it was in the *Manyoshu* collection of poems written in the 8th-century Nara period. This ancient nuance has been revived as an expression of adoration for innocent girls as fresh as a flower bud.

The most frequent objects of *moe* are characters from anime, manga, and games. When otaku get *moe* over girls, they want to protect them. Flesh-and-blood idols can become the object of *moe* too. Fans of Hello! Project often say, using cute little Natsumi Abe's nickname, "I get *moe* from Nacchi!"

Sometime *moe* is not for a person or a character at all. If you get excited by French-maid costumes, then you have "Maid *moe*." If shrine maidens are your thing, there's "Miko *moe*." Other varieties include "Bunny-girl *moe*," "Cat-ear-girl *moe*," and "Eyeglasses-girl *moe*." However, these variables are

clearly sexual fetishes, and there is some criticism that this usage differs from the original ideal of *moe* as something pure, innocent, and fresh.

Some people might conclude that *moe* suggests pedophilia. Certainly, Gal games have a lot of sex in them, and there are dojinshi sold at Comiket full of 2D raping and forced enemas. However, virginity is essential to *moe*. Once actual sex is portrayed, the fantasy is destroyed.

For instance, in the sex game Kanon, the users became *moe* over a brave heroine like Cosette from *Les Miserables* or Pollyanna. Kanon sold even better when a platonic version was released.

Another generator of *moe* for otaku now is the TV anime *Maria-sama ga Miteru (Mother Mary's Watching You)*, which is based on a novel about girls in a Catholic high school. Naturally, neither men nor sex is featured. Otaku guys fantasize about living in a girls-only world, like *Little Women*.

Otaku are especially fond of

the younger-sister *moe* scenario, where the ultimate object of desire is to protect innocence and virginity. Such qualities are prized on the one hand, and continually destroyed with the other hand in masturbatory fantasy, creating an infinite loop of arousal.

In 2004, Kadokawa Shoten, publisher of the anime magazine *Newtype*, started another best-selling magazine called *Shukan Watashi no Oniichan* (*My Big Brother*) to cater to the "younger-sister-*moe*" audience. Every issue of the magazine comes with a plastic action figure attached that depicts something like an elementary school girl exercising in bloomers or swimming in the school pool. The tag line for the mag is "It's not love, or a dream."

Otaku who seek out increasingly untouchable taboos are getting *moe* for Mako-sama, Princess Mako Akishinonomiya, the twelve-year-old daughter of the

second prince in the imperial family. If you search on the Internet, you can easily find comics with Princess Mako as the heroine and even adult comics with Princesses Mako and Kako as little girl lesbians (although they are deleted quickly after being posted).

Then there is NEVADA-*moe*. A photo of a sixth-grade girl who killed her friend with a craft knife to the neck was leaked over the Internet. She was a pretty girl; the logo on her T-shirt read "NEVADA," and a cult of fans soon followed.

Does this sound insane? Maybe. But the taste of *moe* has spread all over Japan. In 2003, Sansai Books published *Moe Tan* (see photo on this page), a study guide to help with memorizing English words through the power of *moe*. It was a best-seller. Surprisingly, it was even sold at colleges as a reference book.

Between its covers, a pretty little anime-style girl name "Ink" (who is supposed to be seventeen years old due to legal considerations, but looks like an elementary school girl) teaches you English with her panties poking out from under her miniskirt. Following this book, *Moeru Korean* and *Yaoi Tan* (for high school girls) were put on the market.

In Japan, you will see flyers and posters with *moe* characters for escort clubs and massage parlors. Even on a train, a typical *moe* anime girl talks to you from a TV monitor. Everywhere, *moe* girls smile at you, just like Big Brother in George Orwell's *1984*. ₴

—By Tomohiro Machiyama

IDOLS

They sing! They dance!
They like to eat and shop!
Be they false or otherwise,
Japanese idols sure are cute.

午後ティー史上
最高おいしい
午後がはじまる。

MORNING MUSUME

A street vendor in Shinjuku hawking Morning Musume girls.

Young adult males mill around the Kosei Nenkin Kaikan theater in small packs, killing time before the idol singer's 5 p.m. show. They munch on junk food and pass around enormous photo books full of their beloved's ever-smiling visage. Two guys have brought a CD boom box, and Aya Matsuura's hit single "Nee?" provides accompaniment as they practice her trademark dance moves (my guess is that the rest of the crowd already knows how to mimic their idol's every move during the show without the need for last-minute rehearsals). After working up a sweat, the pair cools off with plastic Ayaya fans.

It's November 2003. I'm hanging out at the theater in Shinjuku where seventeen-year-old super-idol singer Aya Matsuura (AKA Ayaya) is performing a pair of shows. I tried to get tickets in advance, but they had sold out fast. So I have to settle for the entertainment outside. Luckily, it's quite a sight.

The passion for Miss Matsuura tonight seems single-minded and focused. But

Ayaya is only one part of an enormous family of idol singers and girl groups held together under the collective umbrella known as Hello! Project. And at the center of this maelstrom is a band of attractive young women called Morning Musume ("Morning Daughter") who have recently revolutionized the entertainment industry and given some young men a reason to go on living.

One such person is Kantetsu Nagata. At twenty-four, he is recognized as the leading Morning Musume otaku in Japan. He's even turned his obsession into a profession by becoming a contributing writer to the idol and scandal magazine *Bubka* (see pp.62–63).

We meet at Shinjuku Prince Hotel to talk about Morning Musume and the Hello! Project phenomenon. Kantetsu is friendly, but a bit on the shy side. In classic otaku fashion he's more content to retell the saga of Musume's climb to the top than he is to reveal too much about himself. But that's ok; he tells a pretty good story.

*****

Morning Musume began as five female contestants on an *American Idol*–like TV show called *Asayan*. J-pop musician Tsunku was looking for a new rock lead singer for his band Sharan Q to produce, and the winner of the *Asayan* "audition"

would go from unknown to overnight sensation.

Unfortunately, the five young girls who would later become Morning Musume (Natsumi Abe, Kaori Iida, Yuko Nakazawa, Asuka Fukuda, and Aya Ishiguro) failed to make the grade. But their burning devotion to their collective dream of becoming idol singers endeared them to the viewing public and to the canny Tsunku.

The five losers were given a second chance at stardom. Television cameras followed them as they embarked on a humiliating grassroots campaign to sell 50,000 CDs of their single "Ai no Tane" ("Seed of Love") in five days. Amazingly the daunting feat was accomplished with an extra day to spare. Rechristened "Morning Musume," the girls were signed to Zetima, a subsidy of Sony Music, with Tsunku as their primary producer, composer, and all-around Svengali.

Little of this impressed Kantetsu, at least initially. "I watched the *Asayan* auditions and Morning Musume's early TV appearances. But I wasn't crazy about them. Then I saw their music videos."

The single "Love Machine" was Morning Musume's winter release for 1999. By now, the ranks of the group had swollen to

午後ティー史上
最高おいしい
午後がはじまる。

include eleven members. Their sound had gone from standard-issue J-pop balladry to a dazzling new kind of disco that sampled so many influences (ranging from Okinawan music to the Beatles to the Village People) that even musicologists took notice. The accompanying "Love Machine" promotional clip set the standard for the Musume videos to come and played a key role in helping the CD reach sales in excess of 1.6 million copies. It featured incredible choreography, enough elaborate outfit changes to qualify as cosplay, and visuals that looked like a science-fiction anime come to life.

(Top) "He is willing to die for Ayaya. He is part of a fanatical otaku army, like Al Qaeda."
(Bottom) Two fully-grown men practice their idol's trademark dance moves in public.

Said Kantetsu of the video, "It really shocked me. I'd never seen anything like it before." He was inspired enough to check out a Morning Musume concert in his neighborhood. "Again, I was shocked by what I was seeing and feeling. It was just like the video, but for real." He was hooked for good.

"Now, Morning Musume is a lifestyle," Kantetsu says, and he isn't kidding. Being a real fan also means following related Tsunku acts like Mini-Moni and Tanpopo, who also fall under the massive Hello! Project banner. "There's a concert or an event to attend every three days."

The primary target audience for Hello! Project output is little girls, who feast on the sugary music and the fantasy of being idols themselves. Made up from the shortest members of Morning Musume, Mini-Moni have even provided the voices for the kiddie anime *Hamtaro* and starred in their own partially animated film, *The Great Cake Adventure,* from Toei and Shogakukan.

The lure of Morning Musume for adult men is a far stranger phenomenon. Of course sex appeal is part of it, but that's not enough to explain the unyielding intensity of their devotion.

With so many members and subgroups to keep up with, Morning Musume unfolds like a real-time soap opera or a lengthy manga serial. And as Kantetsu puts it, "When a single doesn't do well, fans blame the agency for making the girls work too hard and exploiting them. The more you follow Morning Musume, the more sympathy you gain for them. The more struggles they endure, the better they become, and the more you like them."

The Japanese have had to coin new words like *moe* (see pp. 50–51) and "Lolicon," for Lolita Complex, to try to understand this mindset where male fans sometimes see themselves as older brothers or father figures to these half-virtual beings. Such notions may have begun on the fringes of anime and manga fandom, but they wound up making millions for companies like Zetima and Sony.

By the end of 2003, even Kantetsu agreed that Morning Musume was going into decline. After increasing the group to include as many as sixteen increasingly younger members, the latest trend has been "graduation" (read: banishment) for the older girls. To add insult to injury, Tsunku and Zetima have been lavishing their devotion of late on a new concoction called Berryz Koubou, whose average member is a ten-year-old girl.

But perhaps the Morning Musume aesthetic, and indeed the whole modern idol industry, has reached its apotheosis with Aya Matsuura.

Imagine Robo Idol: a grinning winking picture of perfection with the humanity

stripped away, whose videos knowingly portray her as a mechanical toy inside a musical box. Ayaya's interests are listed as "sleeping, singing, eating, and shopping." What goes on in her pretty little head beyond that is up to you and millions of other fans to decide (I imagine a really nice-tasting cream filling).

Back at Ayaya's concert in Shinjuku, the afternoon show is just getting out. A long line of happy, satisfied fans comes bouncing out of the hall. By the looks of things, half the crowd comprises little kids and accompanying family members. The other half is guys who remind me of Kantetsu, if only in spirit (he skipped out on tonight's concert to cover an Asami Abe—the kid sister of Morning Musume's Natsumi Abe—event for *Bubka*).

One figure stands out from the throng— a guy clad in an elaborate robe covered in oversized Ayaya photo cards. Even with all the paraphernalia he looks more like a tough young gang leader than the sort of person who'd want to watch some teenage girl sing and dance.

Later, back at the hotel, I show a digital picture of him to Tomo. He reads the delicate embroidery on the back of the robe and tells me, "It means he is willing to die for Ayaya. He is part of a fanatical otaku army, like Al Qaeda."

I want to say something like "Thou Shall Not Worship False Idols," but what would be the point? In Japan, the more false the idol, the better it is. ⥁

午後ティー史上
最高おいしい
午後がはじまる。

Shopping
Prices estimated in US$

Movie Star Pictures
(Top row) Sonny Chiba, Noboru Ando,
Bunta Sugawara,
(Bottom row) Etsuko Shihomi, Bunta
(again), and Meiko Kaji.
$5 each from Marubell Do.

Kaori Iida Trading Cards
Our favorite Morning Musume gal.
$2 each from idol shop Uta Hime Dome in
Nakano Broadway,

Used Pink Lady Bromide Card Wallet
Japan's top idol act of the late seventies.
$20 from Mandarake.

Marubell Do
See map p. 141

Asakusa is cool because it's *anything* but cool. Young people are partying in Roppongi and Shibuya. Those who aren't are most likely having a drink in Shinjuku. And the tourists and old timers? They are in Asakusa Ward, huffing the last few fumes of "old Japan," exchanging money over replica samurai swords.

And tucked away in the Shin-Nakamise Shopping Center in Asakusa is Marubell Do, one of Tokyo's oldest idol shops.

Since 1921, Marubell Do has been selling collectible trading cards of celebrities known as "bromides," a name that comes from a chemical used in film and developing. And it was these bromide cards of popular singers, sumo wrestlers, and silent movie stars that made the first wave of Japanese idol goods. From this Big Bang, idol merchandise evolved into everything a fan could possibly want to own, including posters, buttons, key chains, collectible picture fans, you name it.

Outside of going to a concert or idol event, Harajuku is today the best place to buy such souvenirs. Indeed, it's hard to walk more than a few feet on Harajuku's teen-populated Takeshita-dori strip and not see a shop crowded with trinkets and baubles emblazoned with the latest performers and "talents."

So what does Marubell Do offer that's any different? While they've made concessions to modernity by stocking some Aya Matsuura and Morning Musume goods, Marubell Do's killer app is a vast supply of vintage glamour shots from Japan's Golden Age of celebrities and entertainers.

Enormous files full of 4X8 photos are kept of '70s idol singers like Pink Lady, Junko Sakurada, and Linda Yamamoto. There are also lots of movie stars, from Sonny Chiba (*The Street Fighter, Kill Bill Vol. 1*) to Etsuko Shihomi (AKA Sister Street Fighter) and any number of fair *Godzilla* movie maidens like Kumi Mizuno. Name a trendsetter, a dreamy guy, or a renowned beauty from the 20th century. The odds are Marubell Do's got something on them.

The pictures, which come in both color and black-and-white prints, are organized by last name (so brush up on that hiragana). Just pick the ones you want and the cash register guy will ring them up at around 5 bucks a pop.

Along with the photos are bins full of laminated bromide trading cards,

mostly of big-haired pop acts from the '80s. But every now and then an anime card can be found, usually from something like *City Hunter* or *Saint Seiya*, which once heralded the age of the 2D virtual idol.

But stray too far from the classics, and someone is bound to stage an intervention. For instance, just as I was about to make off with a card of anime icon Space Pirate Captain Harlock, an old lady customer crossed my path and insisted, "I think you should buy some Yuzo Kayama [an Elvis-like crooner from the '60s] photos instead." ⮐

Address: 1-30-6 Asakusa, Taito-ku, Tokyo
Site: http://www.marubell.co.jp/sinnakamise.htm

午後ティー史上
最高おいしい
午後がはじまる。

Hello! Project
Petit Museum Official Shop

Similar to Pleasure Island in "Pinocchio," the Shibuya district functions as a playground for the young. There's no better place to stroll around with your girlfriend, to pummel your face with crepes, and to get the most out of your all-too-brief summer years before you wind up wasting away in a boring job.

Fitting then that Shibuya should also be the home to the official store for Hello! Project, a singing and dancing army of preteen and teenage girls of which the already overpopulated Morning Musume group is only a part.

The Hello! Project shop is located down in the B2 floor of the 109-2 Department Store. Known as the Junior Station, the building is normally inhabited by young ko-gals in training, before they eventually move over to the main 109 store nearby: ground zero for the Japanese "Girls Gone Wild" look.

Since the addition of the Hello! Project shop, 109-2 has been breached by a new type of consumer: obsessive male fans who come to buy buttons, cell phone accessories, photo cards; indeed anything with the object of their adoration's face plastered on it.

They call the place the "Hello! Project Petit Museum," and that's not far from the truth. The walls, which display merchandise behind glass, look more like a gallery exhibit. And if you've ever wondered what actual hardcore idol otaku look like, here's your chance to observe specimens in their natural habitat (or observe *gaijin* like myself observing them).

But be warned: if you want to buy a set of buttons comprising the entire smiley-faced Hello! Project clan, be prepared to spend a massive amount of time. Instead of sim-

Since the Hello! Project store is located in the basement, some of the clientele feels right at home.

ply grabbing what you want and throwing it into a shopping basket, you have to fill out a complex series of forms and hand them over to the store clerk for processing. It's a bit like doing your taxes. I wanted to buy a big old button of Kaori Iida (the tall dumb one) to put on my book bag, but figured I needed to pass a Japanese literacy test before I'd be able to.

If you'd prefer something a little more casual you can always hit the idol shops in nearby Harajuku. But if Shibuya is for young men and women, then Harajuku is for their even younger and more-fashion-conscious siblings, who are bound to make you feel both very old and terribly unstylish. But the smile on your paper or plastic idol's face will never let you down. ₴

Address: Shibuya 109-2 B2F, 1-23-10 Jinnan, Shibuya-ku, Tokyo
Site: http://www.zetima.co.jp/artist/Morning/shop.html

Shopping
Prices estimated in US$

Maki Goto (l) and Kaori Iida (r) Buttons
Only a dozen more to go, and you'll have the whole set.
$1 from a Gachapon machine.

Laminated Kaori Iida Vital Stats Card
Don't leave home without it.
$5 from street vendor at Aya Matsuura concert.

Morning Musume "Go Girl" CD Single
Sadly, not MM's biggest hit (blame their management).
$15.75 from Tower Records.

Morning Musume "Soda! We're Alive" DVD Single
To help memorize the dance steps.
$12.60 from Tsutaya.

Kaori Iida Hardcover Photo Book
At the library, drinking coffee being sprayed with a hose, etc.
$23 from Ali Baba bookstore.

Bubka Magazine

If you run out of cash while in Tokyo, here's a quick (if not easy) way to refill your coffers. Simply track down a well-known idol, snap pictures or film her in compromising positions, and sell the resulting images to *Bubka* magazine for a cool $100,000.

The concept behind *Bubka* is similar to that of sleazy US rags like *Celebrity Skin*: offer cash rewards for candid pics of famous people and print what comes in. But in typical Japanese style, *Bubka* has taken the idea to mind-boggling extremes. Most of the pics come not from professional paparazzi, but from ex-boyfriends and lovers, out to make a fast buck (and possibly exact revenge). One of *Bubka's* most tragic victims was an actress (and I use the term loosely) named Megumi Okina. Her nude photos, taken covertly during a trip to a love hotel with a boyfriend, wound up becoming the key feature of one of *Bubka's* bestselling issues ever.

Indeed, every cheap shot becomes fair play. A 2003 issue of *Bubka* included a free DVD containing more than an hour of footage taken by a hidden camera inside a bathroom stall backstage at a Morning Musume concert.

Along with encouraging readers to stalk idols as they go shopping or undress at the hot spring, *Bubka* will run anything from panty shots and grainy blow-ups of erogenous zones captured from daytime talk shows to high school vacation photos and even Print Club stickers supplied by disgruntled ex-classmates and friends. And if there are still a few pages that need filling, the staff will create an *aikora*, an "Icon Collage" where an innocent's face will be pasted on a porno movie actress's body.

Most Japanese print media try to maintain a good relationship with idol agencies in the hope they will be granted perks like exclusive photo shoots. But despite numerous lawsuits and the occasional arrest (one of the editors took a fall for a Morning Musume *aikora* a few years ago), *Bubka* refuses to play the game. Even so, its influence on the idol world continues to grow.

Shopping
Prices estimated in US$

Pink Lady Bottle Cap Collection
Yours free when you buy Pepsi
or
Get the set from an Akihabara figure
store for $25.

Aya Matsuura "Ne?" DVD single
The greatest idol video of all time? Sho 'nuff. $12 from Tsutaya.

Seiko Matsuda "Kaze Tachinu" CD
1981 album produced by Japan's answer to Phil Spector, Eiichi Otaki. $15.29 from Tower Records.

Kano Sisters Hardcover Photo Book
A pair of hot middle-age idols. Think they've had some work done?
$36 from Kinokuniya Bookstore.

In winter 2003, hard times befell teen singer Asami Abe when *Bubka* printed pictures of her snuggling with a boyfriend. At Abe's next concert, she personally apologized for ruining her virginal image to the very fans who had made the issue a bestseller in the first place. Video footage from this heartwarming moment, taken from a very "interesting" angle, was included in the next issue.

You can buy *Bubka*, or simply browse it, at most convenience stores, including (get this) Family Mart. ⮐

Site: http://www.coremagazine.co.jp/bubka/

*K*araoke is a compound word made up of the Japanese bits for "empty" and "orchestra." Sounds depressing, doesn't it? Well, sometimes it is. Take karaoke in the USA, for example, where local "superstars" live out fantasies of becoming the next American Idol in dingy bars while the clientele talk loudly and gobble peanuts and pretzels.

Meanwhile, in Japan, where the whole thing first got started, karaoke has evolved from a single customized eight-track machine in Kobe City to the modern, monumental "karaoke box."

A karaoke box puts you on center stage for the greatest show on Earth: namely, an exclusive event where you and your pals (and *only* you and your pals) can belt out your favorite anime tunes and pop songs in the sanctuary of a private performance theater (actually more like a room).

It's impossible to leave a train station in central Tokyo without being offered at least one karaoke box venue to choose from.

Simply go inside, kick down for an hourly fee (usually around $10 an hour, but cheaper before peak hours), and rock the mic until you pass out or run out of money. And if all that superstar posturing burns too many calories, then so much the better.

Really massive chains, like Big Echo, are as much restaurants as they are karaoke palaces. Just place an order on the telephone in your room and soon the impeccably dressed staff will be delivering exotic cocktails, heaps of ice cream,

gourmet gratins, and omelets right to your microphone-strewn table.

Meanwhile, bizarrely literal videos bring your favorite song lyrics to life (ever wonder what the Leader of the Pack looked like?), or drown them in frightening '80s hairstyles and fashions.

English songs can be found easily in phone-book-sized catalogs that are standard-issue at most boxes. *Lost in Translation* showed Bill Murray belting out "(What's So Funny 'Bout) Peace and Love and Understanding?" so that should give you some inspiration.

There's an immense number of anime and live-action TV show themes to sing as well. No trip to Tokyo is complete without someone tackling the title track from the *Galaxy Express 999* movie or the original *Kamen Rider* theme ("Rider . . . Punch! Rider . . . Kick!"). But before you go, commit at least one Japanese song to memory that you can use like a tactical weapon to blow your Japanese friends' minds.

Karaoke

Theoretically, if you had enough time and money, you could forgo a hotel room and instead spend your whole tour of duty in Japan inside a karaoke room (the Hello Kitty room, available only at Big Echo, for instance) screaming "Personality Crisis" by the New York Dolls at the top of your lungs.

I actually tried it once, but only lasted about five hours until my vocal chords tuned into guacamole, but hey, that's show business. ⋑

ANIME

Where would we be without Japanese animation? Probably not in Tokyo and someplace else that was really boring instead. Just don't ask why the eyes are so big.

TOEI ANIMATION

A giant monster is about to destroy a balsa-wood skyline. He looks like a cross between an angry steering wheel and a Zulu weapon rack. Eventually, a giant robot will be brought to do him in, but for now the spotlight belongs to the bad guy. While the cameramen sets up the next shot, various grips run around the creature, setting off little smoke pots around him until he's ready for his close-up.

I'm at Toei Studios watching the filming of an episode of *Abaranger*, the latest in the never-ending series that gave birth to the *Power Rangers*.

Toei is one of Japan's biggest media companies and has been involved with film and television since it first formed in the early '50s. And as much as I love watching a guy in a rubber suit mash a miniature version of modern Japan, a look inside the shooting stages is only the appetizer.

Across the street from Toei's Hollywood-sized shooting stages and screening rooms is a rectangular building emblazoned with the smiling face of Puss in Boots, Toei's answer to Mickey Mouse.

Unlike at Disneyland, visitors aren't normally welcomed at Toei's animation department. But thanks to some of Tomo's movie industry connections, I've managed to get a tour of the facility from Manabu Mizuno, a young executive who is the Head of Theatrical Operations for Toei.

Founded in 1956, Toei Animation created Japan's first major color anime feature films. Its annual Manga Matsuri film festivals became required viewing for kids starting in the '60s, a practice that endures to this day. Toei's contributions to television anime are monumental. They include nothing less than the first "magical girl" shows like *Sally the Witch*, "Super Robots" like *Mazinger Z*, and several of the most internationally popular animated shows ever made like *Sailor Moon* and *Dragon Ball Z*.

Puss in Boots lords over the Toei Animation Gallery.

I'm deeply humbled the second I step inside the building. Legendary anime directors like Rintaro (*Metropolis*) and even Hayao Miyazaki (*Spirited Away*) first learned their anime chops at Toei Animation before moving elsewhere or forming their own studios.

Some of my favorite anime, like *Galaxy* Express 999, *Space Pirate Captain Harlock*, and the immortal *Mazinger Z vs. General Darkness*, were made here. And the deeper I walked within its labyrinthine halls, the more I began to feel the history of anime becoming something tangible and real.

*****

Fittingly, the first stop on my Toei tour was the "Animation Gallery," a museum-like space devoted to artifacts from Toei Animation's earliest years. In the gallery were framed animation cells, character sketches, and even 3D models built for Toei's first animated feature, 1958's *Hakujaden (Tale of the White Serpent)*. Toei's original idea, it seemed, was to follow the example of Walt Disney Studios and employ techniques like the filming of live-action actors dressed as characters for artists' reference.

In 1960, Toei made *Saiyuki* (AKA *Alakazam the Great*). Three years later, Osamu Tezuka's Mushi Productions would produce *Tetsuwan Atom*, AKA *Astro Boy*, for television.

Next to the gallery is a showroom full of old, now-antiquated equipment including a huge cumbersome animation camera, an editing flat board, and an optical printer that served Toei for decades,

The long halls of Toei Animation are lined with plaques commemorating each and every single one of its productions. Together, they form a sequential filmstrip of sorts depicting how anime went from a kid's medium to a global phenomenon.

The first major shift happened in the late '70s. While Toei's magical girl and robot shows won the ratings and merchandising wars, a new style of anime was beginning to emerge. In a post–*Star Wars* climate, science fiction anime had the power to attract both mass audiences and hardcore SF fans. Toei's 1979 feature *Galaxy Express 999* was the highest-grossing film of the year in Japan. 1980's *Be Forever Yamato* very nearly trumped *The Empire Strikes Back*.

In the '80s, the anime industry began to notice that the people who were watching anime were getting older and older. Few had expected to find a dedicated adult audience hungry for more animation. Studios began to cater to otaku tastes with direct-to-video productions called OVA (Original Video Animation), which could indulge in heroic doses of sex and violence. Meanwhile, Toei held out on the idea of anime as a children's medium. And it was this quality that made its works

fit to travel around the world to spread the gospel of anime.

* * * * *

Back at Toei Animation, I watch an artist draw the main character from the magical girl show *Tommorow's Nadja* directly onto a small portable computer screen. He uploads it to the network computer where he can immediately compare his work to the storyboard and other drawings in the sequence he's been assigned. Toei first began using this digital ink and paint system known as RETAS in the late '90s. It is what the modern animator slaves over now instead of paper and cells. Toei's public relations department cannot even begin to estimate how much time and money the digital palette has saved.

The Special Effects department, once the domain of the old optical printer, continues the trend of digital domination. In contrast to the somewhat cramped animation pens, the FX room is filled with shiny surfaces and the warm hum of scanners and computer hard drives. Here, folks were working on water effects for a new *One Piece* movie and were adding shimmering falling stars to a new *Saint Seiya* series. Next door, a bank of video equipment is dedicated to digitizing the entire Toei Animation catalog for archival uses and for DVD releases. As I peeked in, the classic wrestling series *Tiger Mask* was being preserved for future generations.

Today, Japan accounts for 60 percent of the world's animated output. Over ninety different anime productions debuted in 2003 and 2004 in Japan alone, and increasing numbers of them will be sold to other countries. Anime is truly a global industry. And yet voices are now emerging that it may soon meet its demise. While there is more money than ever to be made from a hit property, the lion's share goes to licensors, publishers, distributors, and assorted fat cats.

According to the June 3, 2004 issue of the *Mainichi Shinbun*, the average first-year salary for an animator at Studio Ghibli (Hayao Miyazaki's studio and home of the Academy Award–winning *Spirited Away*) is a paltry $20,000 a year.

While a handful of Japanese anime directors like Miyazaki and Mamoru Oshii earn top salaries, the average director earns $40,000 a year. No wonder the labor force is shrinking. Animation schools estimate that 90 percent of their graduates will drop out of the anime industry within five years. Keep in mind though that perilously low

(Top) A diorama of Toei Animation's photography department in the pre-CG days. (Bottom) Toei's now-antiquated animation camera. Note the feather, for wiping dust off the cells.

salaries are more common at smaller studios and are not the norm at larger studios like Toei. Even so, time and labor are eternal problems. Toei's solution has been to outsource. While Toei's classic works were created in-house, the rising cost and volume of production meant that studios in Korea were eventually tapped to supply animation. Recently, Korean studios have raised their prices. Now Toei employs artists in the Philippines and India to supply "in-between" animation. The animation that Toei mainly provides today is "key animation," such as opening, ending, and transformation sequences.

Recently, a government-backed movement has got underway to keep anime as "Japanese" as possible. In 2003 the Ministry of Culture announced that it would provide financial aid to struggling studios and animators; some wonder if it will lead to censorship and control. Clearly, something is deeply wrong with this picture. As anime historian Carl Gustav Horn says, "For a country which taught America the meaning of capitalism in the '80s, the anime industry seems to

have now never heard of it."
Before I walked through the door, I counted on Toei Animation to be a Santa's workshop of creativity. But I began to wonder whatever happened to the spirit

of Japanese animation, the one that helped lead me to Tokyo in the first place. Would simple greed be responsible for the end of anime as a creative medium? Or had the medium simply spent itself after a near-fifty-year run?

(Top) An animator checks out the story-boards in Toei's continuity department. (Middle) Banks of computers digitize the classics for DVD. (Bottom) Original cells and backgrounds for 1959's *Shonen Sarutobi Sasuke*, AKA *Magic Boy.*

I kindly thanked my tour guides and headed back toward the Higashi Oizumi train station. Clouds were gathering overhead and it looked like rain. Then I noticed the video screen on the ticket machine when I finished paying for my ticket: It showed a rendering of a female figure politely bowing in gratitude in a two-frame animated movement.

I finally get it. If this isn't a glimpse of the future of Japanese animation, then what is? The genie has been freed at last from its 2D prison. I wonder what wishes it will choose to grant? ౭

Gundam

In July 2004, Gundam's opened in Osaka. Gundam's is a four-story department store that sells only *Mobile Suit Gundam* products from top to bottom.

Gundam's has Gun-pla (Gundam plastic model kits up to $200), Gundam capsule toys, Gundam snowboards, Gundam wristwatches ($350), Gundam mountain bikes ($600), and Gundam laptop computers ($2,000). No, these are not just toys. Gundam is an established name brand like Chanel or Nike.

Gundam has a bigger fan base than any other anime, but most *Gundam* fans are not anime fans. *Mobile Suit Gundam* in Japan is more like *Star Wars*, *Star Trek*, or *The Lord of the Rings* in the United States.

The Gundam *Universal Century Saga*, which is the original "authentic history" of the franchise and its most popular entry, to date has eleven other Gundam storylines up to the latest entry *Gundam*

Gundam toilet signs from the Bandai Museum. Char Aznable for the guys, and Sayla Mass for the ladies.

Seed. There are also six "side stories" such as *G Gundam*, *Gundam Wing*, and for little kids *SD Gundam*, plus many manga, games, and novels. "Gundam" may have begun as an anime, but it has become independent of the anime boom and established itself as a genre unto itself.

Again, most *Gundam* fans are not anime fans. Many Bishojo characters appear in the *Gundam* stories, but their fans are not getting *moe* from them as they are from other anime. That's because *Gundam*'s star is the robotic Mobile Suit itself.

When the very first *Gundam* was broadcast in 1979, audience ratings were low and the show was canceled. It was not from the anime, but from the plastic models, that *Gundam*'s popularity ignited.

The Mobile Suits that appeared in *Gundam* were nothing like the conventional anime robots of the '70s. The robots were drawn as augmentations of existing military tanks or fighters. The toy company Bandai expanded this idea and sold Gundam scale models with detailed features similar to WWII kits, which were a big hit. Kids and anime fans didn't buy the models, but plastic model and military maniacs did.

Zaku, the villainous Mobile Suit, sold better than the heroic Gundam because Zaku was more like a German battle tank. After modelers became crazy about the Gun-pla, they watched the *Gundam* anime for the first time in reruns. Of course, they liked it, but that doesn't mean they became anime fans.

It was *Gundam*'s hardcore military details that got the fans excited. The battles depicted in *Gundam* were presented as part of a historical war, not as a typical anime story. It was like the Civil War for Americans, the British Fleet for the English, and the Napoleonic Wars for the French.

Japan invaded Asia during World War II, was punished by A-bombs, and after the defeat, forbid itself from possessing offensive armaments through a war-renouncing Constitution. It was unthinkable to yearn for an army in Japan, which was only able to establish a defanged Self-Defense Forces.

Gundam's was the only "good war" that Japanese war enthusiasts could love openly, and they loved the Mobile Suits simply as cool machines, like German Tiger tanks, American F-14 Tomcats, Ford Mustangs, and Harley-Davidson bikes, but not as anime.

One mecca for these fans is the Bandai Museum located in Matsudo, Chiba (see p. 141), east of Tokyo. Another holy place is the town of Kamiigusa in Suginami Ward where the anime studio Sunrise, which created *Gundam*, is based. The studio is not open to public visits, but the fans get choked up with tears of joy just by looking at the *Gundam* banners fluttering in the shopping area around the station.

It's said that *Gundam* fans are the most annoying among various anime fan groups because they've memorized all the dialogue from the first series and quote it all the time. When they beat someone at a game, they sneer and say "This is a Gufu, not a Zaku, stupid!" (the Gufu Mobile Suits are high-performance machines that outclass the Zaku). They don't even care if other people know what they are talking about.

* * * * *

Sunrise is one of over sixty studios in Suginami Ward, located just to the west of Nakano and Shinjuku. Tokyo Movie Shinsha, which created *Lupin the 3rd*, was once located in Suginami Ward, and Studio Ghibli is located in nearby Mitaka. Tools for producing animation, such as cells and equipment from before the CG era, are preserved and exhibited at the Suginami Anime Museum. ₴

—By Tomohiro Machiyama

Suginami Anime Museum: 3-20 Uehagi, Suginami-ku, Tokyo
Tel: Suginami Ward Office 03-3312-2111

Anime Locations
See maps pp. 30, 89

As long as you're visiting Tokyo (or dreaming about it), you might as well tour the places that anime, manga, and special-effects flicks made famous. Sadly, you can't visit some locales, since they never existed in real life. For example, the "maison" apartments of *Maison Ikkoku* were built in the nonexistent Tokyo suburb/ward of Tokeizaka, and you won't find the campus of CLAMP School yet. Fortunately, you can visit some real, but *fictional*, locales—here's a sampling.

* * * * *

Tokyo Tower
Yes, the glorious red knockoff of France's Eiffel Tower. The fact that Tokyo Tower is a cultural landmark building speaks volumes about the lack of cultural landmark buildings in Tokyo. Still, there's no better place in Japan to summon apocalypse upon the world (or save the world from it). Heck, everyone is doing it. Just like in *Magic Knight Rayearth*, tourists (and roving schoolgirl throngs) can go to the eighty-story-high observatory without supernatural leaping or powers of flight. No anime has yet captured one of the Tower's strangest attractions: a wax museum full of movie icons like the xenomorph from *Alien* and rock musicians like Alice Cooper.

Since Tokyo Tower is basically a huge radio antenna, several recording studios are nearby. *Macross Plus* and other anime were recorded in the neighborhood, so don't be surprised if you see your favorite character voice trying to blend in with the crowd on your train.

SEEN IN: *Godzilla, Kimagure Orange Road, Please Save My Earth, Pretty Soldier Sailor Moon, You're Under Arrest, Magic Knight Rayearth, Tenchi Muyo in Love, X, Card Captor Sakura*

How to Get There: 15 minutes from JR's Hamamatsucho Station, 5 from O-Edo subway line's Akabanebashi, 6 from Mita subway line's Onarimon, 7 from Hibya subway line's Kamiyacho

Site: http://www.tokyotower.co.jp/

Shibuya/Harajuku
Whereas the haughty go to gilded Ginza to spend away what remains of Japan's economy, the young go to Shibuya and nearby Harajuku to shop, drink, cosplay, sing karaoke, and rendezvous at love hotels. That's why Shibuya appears in so many movies and series compared to other wards of Japan. Notably, biker Shogo Yahagi careens through the streets around its train station in *Megazone 23*, and the Shibuya 109 shopping monolith rises above the masses below in *The Vision of Escaflowne's* episode 8 flashback and *Comic Party*.

SEEN IN: *Megazone 23, The Vision of Escaflowne, Gals, Comic Party, Paradise Kiss*
How to Get There: Exit from JR's Shibuya Station on the

Yamanote Line and start walking (go to JR's Harajuku Station during the weekends for breathtaking Gothic Lolitas and other cosplayers)

Shinjuku

Shibuya may be where the idle youth go, but Shinjuku has the after-hours entertainment for Japan's miserable salarymen and office ladies. The west side houses the concrete canyons of the Tokyo government offices (most notably seen as Kanoe's lair in *X*), but the east side boasts the Kabuki-cho red-light district (which is naturally where several wild escapades of *City Hunter* and *Get Backers* begin).

SEEN IN: *Demon City Shinjuku, City Hunter, X, Get Backers*

How to Get There: JR's Shinjuku Station on the Yamanote and Chuo lines (see p. 138 for more information on Shinjuku's wild side)

Keio Line and the Tama Hills

After exposing yourself to the twenty-four-hour neon afterglow of Shibuya and Shinjuku, you might want to rest in the suburbs served by the Keio trains. Nestled in the gently rolling terrain of western Tokyo are many anime studios and the area around Seiseki-sakuragaoka Station, the inspiration for *Whisper of the Heart* (and its loose follow-up *The Cat Returns*). Unfortunately, the exact train model seen in *Whisper* has long since retired, but you can still see a few of the sights in the movie, including the huge Keio sign itself.

SEEN IN: *Otaku no Video* (Kichijoji branch), *Heisei Tanuki*

Wars Pompoko, Whisper of the Heart, Cat Returns

How to Get There: From Keio's Shinjuku Station, take the Keio Line to Seiseiki-sakuragaoka Station; to get to Kichijoji Station, transfer from the Keio Line to the Keio's Inokashira Line at Meidai-mae Station (or take the Keio's Inokashira Line directly to Kichijoji from Shibuya Station)

Kamakura

This city south of Tokyo, which was the historical capital of Japan back in the 12th century, is a tourist trap not only for foreigners, but for natives seeking the Daibutsu (literally, "big Buddha" statue), the shrines, and the surfable beachfront. It also happens to be the home of the *Slam Dunk!* basketball drama, although you'll see little of the real Kamakura in that. You will see plenty to remind of you of *Escaflowne* if you take the Enoden train line. In fact, Kamakura-koko-mae Eki ("The Station in Front of Kamakura High School") is the exact place where *Escaflowne* reaches its bittersweet ending. . . .

Cameos: *Slam Dunk!, The Vision of Escaflowne*

How to Get There: From JR's Tokyo Station, take the Yokosuka Line to Kamakura Station; from JR's Shinjuku Station, take the Shonan Shinjuku Line either directly to Kamakura or transfer onto the Yokosuka Line at Ofuna Station; at Kamakura, take the Enoden Line to get around town

Site: http://www.city.kamakura.kanagawa.jp/english/

Yokohama

The harbor town of Yokohama just south of

Tokyo is a popular mini-getaway for Tokyoites seeking shopping and Chinese gourmet pleasures. A mix of European and Asian influences, it's a popular dating spot for people who'd like to visit a foreign country and still be able to take a quick train ride home. It's no surprise that the anime *Yokohama Shopping Trip* and *Macross* (with the Chinese/Japanese menu girl Lynn Minmay) "shoots" here. You can even see the Marine Tower showcased in *Macross*. (Granted, Minmay actually points out the *New* Marine Tower that was supposedly built in 1993—it's a little behind schedule. . . .)

Cameos: *Super Dimensional Fortress Macross, Yokohama Shopping Trip, Aim for the Ace!* (live action), *Sailor Moon* (live action)

How to Get There: How to Get There: From JR's Tokyo or Shinagawa Station, take the Keihin-Tohoku Line to Yokohama Station; from Tokyo's Shibuya Station, take the Tokyu Toyoko Line to Yokohama Station

Site: http://www.city.yokohama.jp/en/

Big Sight and Odaiba

Odaiba is Tokyo's waterfront. There you will find Big Sight, an inverted-pyramid modern art piece/exhibition hall so (in)famous for Comiket and other city-emptying events. (See p. 116.) So it's no surprise that the really inbred anime/manga parodies like *Komugi* and *Comic Party* showcase it. (Sadly, *Otaku no Video* took place before Comiket moved here.) You gotta love any building that transforms into a robot in *Komugi*. . . .

SEEN IN: *Komugi, Comic Party, Bakuryu Sentai Abaranger*

How to Get There: Take the Yurikamome Line from Shinbashi Station to Kokusai-Tenjijo Seimon (check out the other stations for the Fuji TV building, Sega Joypolis, and other amusement parks on the Odaiba artificial island)

Off the Beaten Path

Naturally, we can't cover all the locales that have been in front of the camera, but we can give the more adventurous some resources. The Nationwide Location Site Guide (Zenkoku Roke-chi Gaido) is an all-Japanese website that obsessively lists the locales spotted in everything live-action, from soapy trendy dramas to the latest *Masked Rider* and *Sentai* incarnations. So here's your chance to re-create your favorite live-action *Sailor Moon* episode.

Site: http://joe.ash.jp/travel/loca/

* * * * *

Speaking of places off the beaten path, did you know that even the spaceship in *Super Dimensional Fortress Macross* crashed in Tokyo? The ship landed on South Ataria Island, the fictional name for "the southernmost tip of the Ogasawara Islands" (the same islands of *Godzilla* fame). It's a sulfuric island that is a full 1,100 kilometers (700 miles) from the Tokyo Government Building, but still considered part of Tokyo itself! ₴

—By Egan Loo

Time and money are two of your most precious commodities while running amok around Tokyo on an otaku shopping spree. You don't want to waste a single measurable unit of either. But with all that dashing about from station to station, you're still bound to get a little hungry from time to time. The perfect solution: fast food.

As they did on the rest of planet Earth, chain restaurants like McDonald's and Kentucky Fried Chicken took over Japan decades ago. Before you start complaining that you've already had a bellyful of Big Macs and Popcorn Chicken at home and abroad, keep in mind that the Japanese menus have a few surprises worth noting on them.

Some will tell you to spread for Kobe beef while in Dai Nippon. I'm going to tell you to try something *really far out* like the Teriyaki McBurger (imagine a Quarter Pounder smothered in sugar-based soy sauce) or the Fish McDippers with wasabi sauce. Chicken items are hit and miss on the McMenu owing to recent bird flu scares, but you can still risk Mad Cow disease to your heart's content, or even retreat into the comfort of a creamy McCorn Soup.

Over at Kentucky Fried Chicken, you'll be greeted by a life-sized statue of Colonel Sanders (usually dressed up like Santa Claus around Xmas), who offers you food that's possibly *even greasier* than its American counterpart.

Even if the food alone isn't much a draw for you, it's still worth a peek inside to see how Japan has adopted foreign models of commerce. A lunchtime rush at a Japanese McDonald's is a model of "fast, friendly

BREAK

(This page) The McDonald's in Kabuki-cho has a statue of the Beatles. Don't ask why. (Opposite) The hamburger sez, "This sauce really satisfied my appetite. Mos burger $2.90." (Top) Typical Mos Burger storefront, what the Col. really wants for Xmas is some customers, and the Onigiri Burger.

service" that probably has McDonald's founder Ray Kroc beaming down from heaven daily.

Japanese McDonald's are also killer people-watching spots. There's a pretty young woman toying with her cell phone and shoveling in French fries with her left hand. A pokerfaced businessman barely touches his coffee and watches a Supersized wide-screen TV playing the video for the Christina Aguilera song "Dirrty." A frightening-looking cardboard cutout of famed hamburger clown Ronarudo Makudonarudo surveys his works over by the trash bins.

After comparing and contrasting Japan-US franchises, real adventurous types may also want to check out the bounty of fast food that's yet to leave the Land of the Rising Sun . . . sometimes with good reason.

Japanese friends of mine swear by a chain called Mos Burger, but the meal I had in Kabuki-cho was smothered in lukewarm tomato sauces and served up on an increasingly soggy bun (fittingly, ex–Sex Pistol John Lydon, AKA Johnny Rotten, is said to be a fan of these ill-named burgers). Breakfast at Mos, however, was a pleasant experience, complete with light and fluffy pancakes and the winsome sight of snoozing businessmen trying to get a few winks in before waddling down to the office. I can't even guess what the food at First Kitchen was supposed to taste like; the Shinjuku location appeared to be some kind of clubhouse for chain smokers.

Sometimes you have to risk it all. Secondhand smoke. Food that can kill you or just make you wish you were dead. Just think of all the time and money you'll save! ☙

Fast Food

Mondo Tokyo:
AKIHABARA

Exiting the Akihabara train station is like that moment in the *Wizard of Oz* when a drab black-and-white world suddenly erupts into Technicolor.

Seconds after walking through the turnstiles, you are assaulted by posters, billboards even, advertising the latest video games, manga, and anime releases. Theme songs permeate the air around the "Character Entertainment Shop" Gamers where pedestrians must pass through a gauntlet of cardboard cut out *Gal* game characters and colossal *Gundam* robots. Any path from this point on will take you to some kind of otaku pursuit (although you'll want to consult the Akihabara maps on pp. 84–87 for maximum efficiency).

Across the street from Akihabara Station is the eight-story Radio Kaikan building, home to the K-Books manga and dojinshi superstore and the Kaiyodo

toys show-room. The entire structure is tightly packed with Gachapon machines and stores specializing in figures, comics, and model kits.

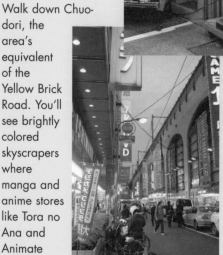

Walk down Chuo-dori, the area's equivalent of the Yellow Brick Road. You'll see brightly colored skyscrapers where manga and anime stores like Tora no Ana and Animate make their home. Erotic, sometimes outright obscene, fliers for PC Gal games barely provoke a blush from the throngs of people here, local otaku so specialized they have their own nickname

from the disapproving straight world: "Akiba Kids."

Meanwhile, Akihabara's neon signs and myriad displays repeat an endless mantra of sorts: Figure. Hobby. Used DVD. Video. Movie. Game Soft. Gundam. TV Games.

Akihabara is often still referred to by its old handle "Electric Town." But today, it's more like a Times Square or Vegas strip for otaku. This is Neo Tokyo: where private fantasy and obsession start to take over an entire city.

Tomo breaks down the archeological detail of the area like this: "The first stage of Akihabara belonged to junk shops. People collected and recycled electronic parts and mechanical things. Those recycled parts were then sold at a cheaper price, and that's what originally made Akihabara a place to buy discount electronics."

As the economy exploded Akihabara became the place to buy dazzling new consumer goods like washing machines, TV sets, camera, and hi-fi equipment at discount prices. This incarnation of Electric Town persisted until massive chain stores like Yodobashi and Bic Camera, the Japanese equivalent of Circuit City or Best Buy, began popping up in other

wards and in the suburbs. Akihabara began losing its patrons. However, in the '80s, the magazine *Radio Life* (see p. 90) ignited a new underground hacker boom. Akihabara got a second wind from the sales of illegal electronic devices like mini cameras, radio scanners, eavesdropping devices, and bootleg software. Such goodies had always been for sale in Akihabara, but now they became its bread and butter. The straight folks were gone, and the nerds took over. They decided to

make it an otaku paradise.

* * * * *

As the '90s rolled around, advances in digital encryption began to put the kibosh on pursuits like radio scanning and hacking. But the computer world gave something back to the otaku: Gal games—girlfriend and sex simulators that chain stores wouldn't dare carry. The over-eighteen crowd could buy them by the stacks in Akihabara, and the stores began to offer other otaku goods like figures, dojinshi, dojin soft, and anime that was decidedly not suitable for the kiddies. Recently, a host of cosplay cafés (like Mailish, see p. 113) have opened where otaku can enjoy food and conversation with girls

dressed as anime characters.

As much as anime, manga, and games dominate the area, there are still lots of ways to access the old-style Akihabara. Right around the corner from the station is the Radio Center (easily identified by its endearingly goofy *Star Wars*–era robot and spaceship mural), a maze of corridors where individual dealers sell every possible kind of tiny electric gadget, from individual electric lights and fiber optic cables to spy cameras and stun guns disguised as cell phones.

There're also the "junk shops" that line the side streets and alleyways where enormous plastic bins full of random assortments of dirt cheap knickknacks: video cards, blank media, batteries, and "what the hell?" items like giant rubber comedy ears.

Of course, big chain electronic stores are still

here, some offering "Duty-Free Shopping" and English-speaking staff members to woo the tourists. But I make sure to steer clear of such places. On my first trip to Akihabara, I tried to buy a palm-sized TV and was nearly lured into a scary passport scam before I bailed out of the transaction altogether (later, I found out the place was a front for the Russian Mafia).

A few years later, my cell

phone got lost somewhere inside the massive, imposing Radio Kaikan. I imagined some evil otaku hacking every last bit of personal data out of it as I started to retrace my steps. Over in the dirty dojinshi section of K-Books, one of the clerks handed my phone over. He said one of the customers had found it and graciously turned it in.

Let the local salarymen and office ladies say what they want about otaku, their awkwardness, and their weird antisocial ways. Akihabara is a messy nerd's room writ large, and the "Akiba Kids" are all right. ⮐

MAP

Tokyo's electric town, a haven for hackers, and a messy otaku's room writ large, Akihabara is the heart of the Anime City. Here's what you'll find there.

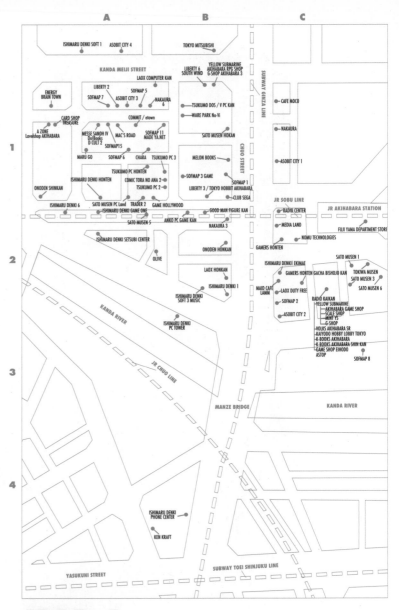

HOBBY SHOPS

Asobit City 2
03-3251-3100 / MAP-1 C3
Model trains, figures, character goods, games, Gundam, books, DVD.

Asobit City 4
03-5209-2311 / MAP-1 A1
Air guns, military goods.

Animate Akihabara
03-5209-3330 / MAP-2 C4
Character goods, DVD, CD, manga, books, dojinshi, telephone cards, trading cards.

K-Books Akihabara
03-3255-4866 / MAP-1 C2
Telephone cards, trading cards, CD, DVD, VHS, animation cells, dolls, cosplay, manga, books, anime, dojinshi.

Fujiyama
03-3251-2161 / MAP-1 C2
Manga, game software, Gundam kits, figures, character goods, train models.

Yamagiwa Soft Kan
(currently remodeling after a fire)
03-5256-3300 / MAP-2 B4
CD, DVD, consumer games, PC games, character goods.

MOVIES, MUSIC, & SOFTWARE (AKA "SOFT")

Ishimaru Denki Honten
03-3255-1500 / MAP-1 A2
CD, DVD, PC, PC soft, consumer electric goods.

Ishimaru Denki Soft 1
03-3251-5555 / MAP-1 A1
CD, DVD, game soft, PC soft.

Ishimaru Denki Soft 3 Music
03-3257-1300 / MAP-1 B2
CD, DVD.

Ishimaru Denki 6
03-3255-1500 / MAP-1 A2
DVD soft, video.

Yamagiwa Soft Anime Kan
MAP-2 C4
Anime CDs, DVD, Bishojo games.

Yamagiwa Soft Eizo Kan
MAP-2 C4
DVD, videos, LD.

Yamagiwa 98 Navi Shop C
MAP-2 C4
DVD, CD, LD.

Yamagiwa U-Shop 1, 2
MAP-2 B4, C4
DVD, CD, LD

Liberty 1, 2, 3
MAP-2 C3, MAP-1 A1, MAP-1 B2
Used CD, DVD, LD, video.

Liberty 4
03-5294-6170 / MAP-2 C3
Used CD, DVD, LD, video, telephone cards, game soft, dojinshi.

Liberty 5
03-3253-5686 / MAP-2 C3
Used CD, DVD, LD, video, figures, game soft.

Liberty 6
03-3257-3451 / MAP-1 B1
Used CD, DVD, LD, video, telephone cards, manga, dojinshi.

Spot
03-5256-1664 / MAP-2 A2
CD, DVD, capsule & omake toys.

GAMES

Asobit City 1
03-3251-3100 / MAP-1 C1
PC games.

Ishimaru Denki Game One
03-3251-0011 / MAP-1 A2
Game hardware and soft, character goods, DVD.

MAP-1

Soft Land Pochi
03-3255-0056 / MAP-2 B3
Used game machines, PC games, and cell phone games.

Softmap Honten
0077-78-8686 / MAP-2 B3
Used and new Windows games, used DVD, anime.

Softmap 3 Game
0077-78-8686 / MAP-1 B2
New and used games, DVDs, used Windows games (adults and all-ages).

Softmap 4
0077-78-8686 / MAP-2 C3
Anime and game soft.

Messe Sano Honten
03-3255-3452 / MAP-2 B3
Game machines, character goods, and import games, dojin soft.

Akibang 2
03-5298-2565 / MAP-2 A4
CD-R media, DVD, game- related goods, dojin soft.

Tokiwa Musen
03-3253-8768 / MAP-1 C2
Game machines, game-related goods.

Astop
03-5256-5911 / MAP-1 C2
Game machines, cell phones, PDA.

Media Land Akihabara
03-3251-7004 / MAP-1 C2
New and used game soft, and game hardware, trading cards, dojin soft.

Game Hollywood
03-5297-3281 / MAP-1 B2
Imported game machines and software, magazines.

Macs Road Honten
03-5256-2925 / MAP-1 A1
Used PCs, used PC soft, used game soft.

Trader
03-3255-3493 / MAP-2 B3
Used games.

Trader 2
03-3255-0777 / MAP-1 A2
Used games, DVD.

Game Arc Mega Shop
03-3255-7644 / MAP-2 B3
Non-Japanese games, game goods.

Furukawa Denki
03-3251-3022 / MAP-2 B3
Games, Bishojo games, dojin soft.

Friends
03-5812-2471 / MAP-2 B1
Used games, game goods.

BISHOJO GAMES

Asobit City 3
03-3253-0761 / MAP-1 A1
Adult PC games.

Anko PC Game Kan
03-3257-2535 / MAP-1 B2

Game machines, PC games, PC goods, cell phones.

Gamers Honten
03-5298-8720 / MAP-1 C2
Books, CD, DVD, games, goods, trading cards for "BROCCOLI."

Gamers Honten Gacha Bishojo Kan
03-5298-2015 / MAP-2 C2
Gachapon and Bishojo, section for "BROCCOLI."

Softmap 14
0077-78-8686 / MAP-2 B2
Windows game soft, DVD, related goods.

Emania
03-5209-2420 / MAP-2 B3
Bishojo games.

Nakaura 3
03-3257-2471 / MAP-1 B2
Bishojo games, adult games, home electronics.

Messe Sanoh V
03-3255-3442 / MAP-2 B3
Bishojo games, anime DVDs.

Messe Sanoh V Bekkan
03-3255-3453 / MAP-2 B1
Bishojo games, event floor.

Game Shop Eihodo
03-3255-6700 / MAP-1 C2
Bishojo games, DVD.

Ware Park Na-Vi
03-3257-6136 / MAP-1 B1
Bishojo games, dojin soft, trading cards, anime DVDs.

Made Ya.Net
03-3253-5100 / MAP-1 B1
Bishojo games, anime DVD, adult DVD, music CDs.

Soft Club Pasomaru
03-5294-6085 / MAP-2 B4
Games, Bishojo games, DVD.

Nekomimi Ya
03-5294-1338 / MAP-2 A3
New Bishojo games.

Getchu Ya
03-3257-3003 / MAP-2 B2
Bishojo games, character goods.

GAME BOARDS

Phantom
03-3257-1126 / MAP-2 A4
Arcade game boards. Related goods.

Try
03-5295-0667 / MAP-2 B3
Arcade game boards. Related goods.

Mac Japan
03-3255-0737 / MAP-2 B3
Arcade game boards. Related goods.

G-Front
03-5807-1685 / MAP-2 B1
Arcade game boards. Related goods. Bishojo games.

G-Front Shinten
03-5209-3420 / MAP-2 C1
Arcade game boards. Related goods. Bishojo games.

MANGA

Comic Tora No Ana 2
03-5256-2055 / MAP-1 A1
New manga, new adult manga, new dojinshi, and illustration books.

K-Books Akihabara Shin Kan
03-5297-5065 / MAP-1 C2
New manga, magazines, dojinshi, dojin soft.

Tachibana Shoten
03-3251-6324 / MAP-2 B4
Manga, dojinshi, dojin soft, and adult DVDs.

Brains Town
03-5298-2433 / MAP-1 A1
Manga, magazines,and Bishojo manga.

Do! Books
03-5289-8460 / MAP-1 A1
Bishojo manga, regular manga, magazines, illustration books, adult anime.

Sangatsu Usagi
03-3252-5522 / MAP-2 B3
Used PC, DVD, imported comics, character goods.

DOJINSHI/ DOJIN SOFT

Akibao 4
03-5207-6226 / MAP-2 B4
Dojin soft, dojin goods, dojinshi.

Comic Tora no Ana 1
03-5256-2838 / MAP-2 C3
Dojinshi, dojin soft, dojin goods, figures, Gundam kits, trading cards.

Messe Sanoh III, IV
03-3255-3064 / MAP-2 B3, MAP-1 A1
Dojinshi, dojin soft.

D Cult 2
03-5207-6755 / MAP-1 A1
Dojinshi, dojin soft.

Mandarake Dojin Kan
03-3252-7007 / MAP-2 B4
Dojinshi for men, Bishojo manga, animation cells, toys, trading cards.

Manga Okoku
03-5297-8395 / MAP-2 B3
Dojinshi, dojin soft, telephone cards.

White Canvas
03-5298-8270 / MAP-2 B2
Dojinshi, dojin soft, dojin goods, CD-R media.

Melon Books
MAP-1 B1
Manga, dojinshi, dojin soft, trading cards, figures, DVD.

FIGURES / GARAGE KITS / PLASTIC MODELS / DOLLS

Yellow Submarine Scale Shop
03-5298-7712 / MAP-1 C2
Scale models, tools, modeling tools, and books.

Yellow Submarine Historical Figure
03-5298-7712 / MAP-1 C2
Historical figures, related goods.

Yellow Submarine G-Shop
03-5298-3123 / MAP-1 C2
Garage kits, plastic models, capsule toys, *omake*, character figures, tools.

Yellow Submarine G-Shop 2
03-5289-9003 / MAP-2 B2
Garage kits, plastic models, capsule toys, *omake*, character figures, rental showcases.

Yellow Submarine G-Shop 3
03-5297-5400 / MAP-1 B1
Garage kits, plastic models, capsule toys, *omake*, and character figures.

Kaiyodo Hobby Lobby Tokyo
03-3253-1951 / MAP-1 C2
Character figures, soft vinyl action figures, *omake* goods.

Volks Akihabara Sr
03-5295-8160 / MAP-1 C2
Garage kits, action figures, Gundam kits, dolls, books, tools.

Liberty 7
03-5209-7422 / MAP-2 C3
Figures, toys, plastic models.

Nomu Technologies
03-3253-8782 / MAP-1 C2
Military figures, scale models.

Goodman Figure Kan
03-3251-3557 / MAP-1 B2
Imported toys, action figures, trading cards, soft vinyl toys.

Tokyo Hobbit Akihabara
03-5209-4111 / MAP-1 B2
Garage kits, figures, tools, materials, character toys.

Azone Label Shop Akihabara
03-3252-8855 / MAP-1 A1
Dolls, clothes for dolls.

Hobby Shop Kotobukiya
03-3257-2360 / MAP-2 B3
Figures, garage kits, Gundam kits, dolls, tools.

Hobby Shop Flyer
03-5295-0046 / MAP-2 B3
Antique toys, toys, action figures, toys.

Pord
03-5209-6664 / MAP-2 B2
Capsule toys, *omake*, rental showcases.

Figure Shop Mint Akihabara
03-3254-0522 / MAP-2 C2
Figures, dolls, action figures.

TRADING CARDS/ CHARACTER GOODS

Yellow Submarine Game Shop
03-3526-3828 / MAP-1 C2.
Trading cards, trading card games, card goods.

Yellow Submarine Mint Ys
03-5289-7762 / MAP-1 C2
Trading cards (sports / idols)

Yellow Submarine Magickers
03-5207-5053 / MAP-2 B3
Trading card games, card-related goods.

Yellow Submarine Duel Center
03-5289-7671 / MAP-2 B3
Shop devoted to DuelMasters trading card game.

Chara
03-5256-0423 / MAP-1 A1
Trading cards, telephone cards, figures, character goods, garage kits.

Yellow Submarine RPG-Shop
03-5297-5402 / MAP-1 B1
RPGs, board games.

Gamers Honten 3
03-5298-2015 / MAP-1 C2
Gachapon, UFO catchers, trading cards.

Chime
03-5298-3466 / MAP-2 B3
Trading cards, posters, dojinshi, character goods.

Anime Shop Get
03-5297-3697 / MAP-2 B2
Trading cards, telephone cards, dojinshi, Bishojo games.

Anime Shop Cosmit
03-3257-8815 / MAP-1 A1
Trading cards, animation cells, capsule toys, character goods.

Hobby King Yume Ya
03-3526-3357 / MAP-2 A2
Trading cards, figures, characters goods, event space.

Card Shop Treasure
03-3526-4611 / MAP-1 A1
Telephone cards.

COSPLAY

Cospa Shop
03-3526-6877 / MAP-2 B2
Cosplay, character clothing, character goods.

Olive
03-5256-0010 / MAP-1 A2
Cosplay clothing,

Energy
03-3526-5877 / MAP-1 A1
Cosplay clothing.

HOBBY

Hobby Land Pochi 2
03-5256-2721 / MAP-2 B3
Model trains, train-related items.

Tsukumo Robokon Magazine Kan
03-3251-0987 / MAP-2 A4
Robots, robot-related goods.

Echigoya Tokyo
03-5209-7202 / MAP-2 B1
Air guns, electric guns, plastic guns, figures.

ELECTRIC GOODS

Ishimaru Denki 1
03-3257-1100 / MAP-1 B2
PCs, PC soft, home electronics, cell phones.

Ishimaru Denki Phone Center
03-3251-0800 / MAP-1 B4
Cell phones, PHS, telephones, FAX.

Ishimaru Denki Ekimae
03-3255-1600 / MAP-1 C2
Home electronics, PCs, PC soft.

Ishimaru Denki Setsubi Center
03-32563-3221 / MAP-1 A2
Air conditioners, security cameras.

Nakaura Honten
03-3257-2411 / MAP-1 C1
Home electronics, PCs, duty-free goods.

INTERNET/COSPLAY CAFÉ

Pronto
03-5209-6760 / MAP-2 B4
Internet café, wireless LAN.

Kissa Toyo
03-3258-6868 / MAPS2 C3
Internet café.

Cafe Moco
MAP-1 C1
Internet café.

Mailish
http://www.mailish.jp / MAP-2 A2
Internet café. See p. 113.

Cure Maid Cafe
http://www.curemaid.jp / MAP-2 B2
Maid cosplay café.

Cos-Cha
http://www.cos-cha.com / MAP-2 A2
Maid cosplay café.

Maid Cafe Lamm
http://www.lammtarra.com/cafe / MAP-1 C2
Maid cosplay café.

PC & ELECTRONICS

Laox Honkan
03-3253-7111 / MAP-1 B2
Home electronics, PCs, and duty-free section.

Laox Computer Kan
03-5256-3111 / MAP-1 B2
Computer store.

Onoden Honkan / Shinkan
MAP-1 A1, B2
Home electronics.

Sato Musen
03-3253-5871 / MAP-1 A1-2, B1-2, C2
Home electronics. PCs.

Radio Center
03-3251-0614 / MAP-1 C2
Electronics, gadgets, and spare parts since 1945.

Akibao 1
03-3251-6727 / MAP-1 A1
DOS, personal computer parts, media-related items, IT supplies, game- related goods.

Akibao 3
03-3257-0235 / MAPS2 B4
CD-R media, game-related goods, DOS.

MAP-2

Map labels (MAP-2):

SUBWAY GINZA LINE
SUBWAY CHIYODA LINE
SUBWAY GINZA LINE
SUHEICHO STATION
KURAMAE BASHI STREET
TUSMAGOI HILL
G-FRONT
FRIENDS
SEGAFREDO
ECHIGOYA TOKYO
MESSE SANO V BEKKAN
HOBBY KING YUME YA
G-FRONT / FIGURE SHOP MINT
GAMERS 1
COS-CHA
GETCHUU YA
Mailish
SPOT
HOBBY LAND POCHI 5
CURE MAID CAFE
UCHUSEN
PORO
COSPA SHOP
AKIHABARA GACHAPON KAIKAN
WHITE CANVAS
YELLOW SUBMARINE G-SHOP 2nd
SOFMAP 14
ANIME SHOP GET
LIBERTY 7
emania
TRADER
LIBERTY 5
OVERTOP II
SANGATSU USAGI
T-ZONE AKIBA PLACE
YELLOW SUBMARINE
DUEL CENTER
HOBBY LAND POCHI 2
MAC JAPAN
LIBERTY 1
LIBERTY 4
SOFMAP 12
TRY
SOFMAP 9
MANGA OKOKU
SOFMAP 10
SOFT LAND POCHI
CHIME
COMIC TORA NO ANA 1
SOFMAP 4
KISSA TOYO
HOBBY SHOP FLYER
FURUKAWA DENKI
MESSE SANO
TSUKUMO ex.
SOFMAP 13
HOBBY SHOP KOTOBUKIYA
GAME ARC MEGA SHOP
YELLOW SUBMARINE MAGICERS
G-SHOP 2
MAX ROAD 1set
MESSE SANO V
MESSE SANO III
SOFMAP
GAME SHOP KAMI FUSEN
OVER TOP
TACHIBANA SHOTEN
J GAME
TRY AMUSEMENT TOWER
NEKO MIMI YA
AKIBAOU 6
SOFT CLUB PASOMARU / MANDARAKE DOJIN KAN
KAKUTA SOFMAP
ANIMATE AKIHABARA
MIRAGE
AKIBAO 4
PRONTO
ROBOKON MAGAZINE KAN
AKIBANG 2
AKIBAO 5
YAMAGIWA 98 NAVI SHOP C KAN
TSUKUMO 5
AKIBAO 3
piacela
YAMAGIWA SOFT KAN
YAMAGIWA SOFT ANIME KAN
YAMAGIWA SOFT EIZO KAN
PHANTOM
YAMAGIWA U-SHOP 1
YAMAGIWA U-SHOP 2
ISHIMARU DENKI SOFT 1
ASOBIT CITY 4
TOKYO MITSUBISHI
KANDA MEIJI STREET
CHUO STREET

Sofmap 8
0077-78-8686 / MAP-1 C3
Used PCs, new Macintosh, cell phones, PHS.

Sofmap 9
0077-78-8686 / MAP-2 B3
Used Macintosh, computer parts.

Sofmap 10
0077-78-8686 / MAP-1 B3
Synthesizers, MIDI-related items, video-editing- related items.

Sofmap 11
0077-78-8686 / MAP 1B1
Used PDA, digital cameras, mobile PC.

Sofmap 12
0077-78-8686 / MAP-2 C3
Buys used PCs, related items.

Sofmap 13
0077-78-8686 / MAP-2 B3
Computer repair.

Sofmap 15
0077-78-8686 / MAP-1 A1
Buys used PC software.

Kakuta Sofmap
0077-78-8686 / MAP-2 B3
New and used Windows PC, business soft, supplies.

Tsukumo PC Honten
03-3253-5599 / MAP-1 A1
PCs, related items, PDA, business soft.

Tsukumo PC Honten 2
03-3253-5599 / MAP-2 B2
PC parts, used PCs.

Tsukumo PC Honten 3
03-3253-5599 / MAP-1 B1
Cell phone, PHS, cell accessories, LCD screen display.

Tsukumo Dos /V PC Kan
03-3254-3399 / MAP-1 B1
PC, related items, custom PC parts.

Digital Pro Shop Tsukumo 5
03-3251-0531 / MAP-2 A4
Video editing tools, camera goods, networking tools, video stream systems.

Tsukumo ex.
03-5207-5599 / MAP-2 C3
PC parts, cell phone.

T-Zone Akiba Place
03-5209-7501 / MAP-2 B3
Custom PC parts, PC monitors.

Soft Land Pochi
03-3255-9088 / MAP-2 B3
Business soft, Windows games, trading cards, PC hardware.

Nakaura 6
03-3257-2571 / MAP-1 A1
PC junk, AV junk.

Overtop
03-3255-3229 / MAP-2 B3
DOS parts and software.

Overtop 2
03-3255-4038 / MAP-2 B3
DOS parts and software, outlet items.

Akibao 6
03-3257-0234 / MAP-2 B4
DOS, computer parts, PC magazines, car audio, junk.

Ishimaru Denki PC Tower
03-3257-1200 / MAP-1 B3
CD, DVD, PCs, PC soft.

Sofmap 1
0077-78-8686 / MAP-1 B2

Custom-made parts, monitors, PDA, new Windows PCs, PC games, DVD.

Sofmap 2
0077-78-8686 / MAP-1 C2
New Macintosh, printers, scanners, monitors, MIDI, business soft, DVD.

Sofmap 5, 6, 7
0077-78-8686 / MAP-1 A1
Used PC shop. Used monitors. Used notebook PCs.

From pachinko, to pornography, and cell phone scams, there's all kinds of fun to be had. And that's not even counting the arcade.

GAMES

SANSAI BOOKS
INSIDE THE GAME LAB

Hack into your co-worker's computer. Make Trojan horse viruses to take over someone else's PC. Steal personal data from the terminal of an Internet café. Do away with DVD copy protection. Duplicate PlayStation games for fun and profit. Rip off someone's credit card numbers. Watch satellite TV for nothing. Use the phone without ever paying the bill. Retrieve old data from a used digital device. Open any door using a skeleton key. Borrow money from the loan company and never pay it back. Ride the subway as much as you like without ever coughing up a cent.

Do any of these things, and you've broken the law. But merely *tell* someone how to do them? No problem.

And there's a line of magazines in Japan that can hook you up with the right information. Nothing underground about it. A law-abiding major company called Sansai Books distributes its handy digest-sized publications to stores all over the country.

Sansai's founding publication, and the cornerstone of its editorial output, is *Radio Life*. This small digest-sized magazine lists little-known frequencies to listen in on. At the top are police and military frequencies and codes to crack. Then there are a million civilian devices to listen to, including cordless telephones and wireless microphones used by idol singers.

B-Geeks is Sansai's PC magazine, a mix of raw computer code and do-it-yourself articles like "How to Retrieve Erased Data from Rental Digital Cameras." *URATTU!* (which means "outfoxing") is a grab bag of techniques for reading the bar codes on candy-toy packages (to get the prizes you want), con games, moneymaking schemes, pachinko-machine hacking methods, and tips on how to pick up women using message boards, chat rooms, and cell phones.

Keep in mind that these aren't underground publications by a long shot; Sansai's titles are sold in bookstores across Japan. Its most popular publication is *Game Lab*, which boasts a monthly circulation of 200,000 copies. *Game Lab* has not only the expected "tips and tricks" section, but also detailed information on how to pirate games, crack copy protection, hack on-line communities, and modify consumer electronics into Frankenstein monsters.

Sansai's offices contain the usual editorial work pens as well as large tables loaded down with computer parts, AV equipment, and piles of software. The casing of a Sony PlayStation2 lies cracked open next to a screwdriver and a soldering iron. Nearby, a Microsoft Xbox has been stripped down to the motherboard and is framed by a stack of DVD-Rs. For technophiles, it would be hard to imagine a cooler place to work.

Yet as Sansai editor Hiroyuki Watanabe points out, "A lot of readers write asking for jobs here, but they rarely have what it takes. The most important thing you need is physical stamina, because the hours are long with very little sleep. The next is common sense and communication skills. It's not so important that someone who works here knows about computers and technology. You can learn about stuff like that. But you can't be taught these other things."

So where are the

hackers? On the other side of the page. While much of the raw data can be found online, Sansai's mags have become must-buy publications for Japan's hackers, information junkies, and troublemakers. They provide them with a public arena, and to be printed within Sansai pages is a status symbol.

The people who read *Game Lab* grew up with computers, home consoles, and video games of all stripes. They've moved on from playing games to getting jobs in programming, engineering, and security. It's possible that Sansai actually has a secret army at its fingertips, one that could bring Japan to its knees. Instead, *Game Lab* consumers are content to play the game for fun: a race between encryption

Circuit boards, game hardware, mysterious CD-Rs, and crazy magazines are commonplace inside the offices of Sansai Books. There's even a persimmon somewhere in this picture, trust us.

and cracking, and a kind of "cops and robbers" for the 21st century. But you never know what the next level of the game might be, especially in a world where every cell phone is a transmitter, and every person a potential receiver.

After saying good-bye to Watanabe and the Sansai staff, I'm compelled to take a twilight stroll through Akihabara, the birthplace of Japanese hacker culture. But on the surface, all I can see is poker-faced students and salarymen alike scouting the stores for the latest in electronics, video games, and PC soft amusements.

I wander over to the Radio Center, an ancient-yet-high-tech labyrinth of gadgets, adapters, plugs, and cables that's been a staple of Akihabara since the war. It feels like a cross between Q's workshop from *James Bond* and a black market in *Blade Runner*. Wanting to summon the spirit of Sansai Books, I decide to buy a "Telcut," a portable pocket-sized cell phone jammer that blocks incoming and outgoing calls within a fixed radius.

I try it out for the first time on the train platform to kill time. At first, nothing happens. Then slowly, the virus begins to spread. People begin to double-check their phones, looking for signs of life, wondering if they've paid the bill, if service is down, etc. I half expect to see Tokyo turning into glowing columns of green code, like in *The Matrix*. Instead, I switch the Telcut off and begin to plan the best way to sneak it past customs for the flight back. ⮐

Shopping
Prices estimated in US$

Telcut
Portable cell phone jammer. $100 from Akihabara Radio Center.

Compact USB JoyPad
Palm-sized game controller for PC. $5 from Akihabara "junk shop".

Perfect Cherry Blossom
Dojin-soft fan-made videogame. $20 from Tora no Ana.

Azunaburu
Dojin-soft fan-made videogame. $5 from a dealer at Winter Comiket 2003.

Gal Games

Two used Gal games, *Gaku-en* (l) and *Ai Doru* (r). How used? Don't ask.

The categories of video games at Furukawa Denki are familiar to anyone who's ever considered partaking of some adult entertainment: Big Boobs, Lesbians, Nurses, Naughty Schoolgirls and Maids. But instead of silicone-injected human beings, the software boxes and CD jewel cases are decorated with female characters drawn in a big-eyed anime style. And a lot of these characters look young. Like, real young. Tentacles are assaulting some girls, others recline in lascivious poses. Most are covered in unspeakable fluid of some sort.

Whatever happened to Mrs. Pac-Man? I wonder.

It's a nice night in Akihabara, not too cold for November, and I'm inside the dirtiest video game store in the entire world. It is called Furukawa Denki. The size of the store is modest (hey, I didn't say it was the *biggest*), but the interior is packed from

floor to ceiling with a humongous selection of PC games.

Akira Iwasaki is a freelance writer for Sansai Books. He was introduced to me as "the most *moe* guy in Japan," and he has escorted me to Furukawa Denki to show me what generates the pulse of today's Electric Town. It caps off a day of interesting discoveries.

Earlier in the day, Iwasaki and another Sansai scribe, "Junk Hunter" Yoshida ("Call me Junk," he says memorably), sat down to school me on how Japan literally fell in love with a whole new kind of video game.

*****

Every kid with a joy pad and dreams of a high score knows this much: video games really began in Japan in 1978 with Taito's Space Invaders. By the early

'80s, amusement companies like Namco and Nintendo were filling arcades with made-in-Japan games like Pac-Man and Donkey Kong.

While coin-op culture was spreading across the world, a new kind of game was emerging in Japan. Iwasaki pinpoints the moment to 1982, when the Koei Company released Danchi Tsuma no Yuwaku (Seduction of the Condominium Wife) for the PC 8001 home computer. A mix of text-based erotic adventure and crude graphics (literally, owing to the eight-color palette), it was a surprise hit. There was nothing on the market like it. Koei became a major software company, and the bold new era of Bishojo ("Beautiful Girl") games, or Galge (short for "Gal games") had begun.

In 1994 the Konami Company was about to close down for good when fans set up a fund to produce a platonic "romantic simulation" for the PC engine called Tokimeki Memorial. With no sex whatsoever, it became the next best-selling Bishojo game, and put Konami on the map.

In 1999, an independent software development house named Visual Art's/Key published an adult game called Kanon for the Windows PC. In the game, the player meets five girls in a snowy small town and experiences tragic love affairs with them.

Naturally, Kanon was a sex game, and that's what initially attracted male consumers. They wound up reaching for the tissue box all right, but to soak up tears over the emotional trials and tribulations of pure love. Like the readers of girls' comics, men found themselves identifying with the protagonists.

The romance simulator that started it all: 1994's *Tokimeki Memorial—Forever with You.*

Kanon was then released for the PlayStation minus the explicit sex. It sold even better than the dirty PC version did.

The next stop was a Kanon anime, broadcast on network television. The feedback from the then-new Internet was unanimous. Otaku wanted characters *and* smut. Tear jerking to go along with jerking off—a very Gal game concept.

For anyone who would make claims that the whole scenario begins to look alarmingly like child porn, rest assured that the youth protagonists in Galge are technically not minors. Iwasaki points out that the most common defense used by game makers is that the girls are in their late teens and are *just pretending* to be so young. And if that's not convincing enough, then maybe they've got a glandular problem that has stunted their growth.

As floppy discs gave way to CD-ROMs and crude home computers gave way to a succession of Windows operating systems, the Bishojo games evolved into a mix of gorgeously detailed illustrations, full-blown animation, and dazzling computer graphics. Modern games often employ all three techniques.

The visuals of Bishojo games strengthened the links between anime, manga, and the electronics culture of Akihabara Ward. And they created a new otaku industry where a small crew consisting of an illustrator, a scriptwriter, and a programmer could churn out a product that could sell as many as 30,000 copies. With some 500 new Bishojo titles debuting annually, it's estimated that the genre currently accounts for 25 percent of all software sales in Japan.

Paralleling those figures are some other high scores: a million Japanese people may be afflicted with "*hikikomori* syndrome," a new social disease that takes the form of a shut-in lifestyle. Men are avoiding relationships in increasing numbers. Marriage rates are declining, along with birthrates. Japan currently ranks dead last among countries in the frequency of sexual intercourse. But I'm willing to guess they'd also rank number one in the field of virtual sex.

Iwasaki and Junk Hunter both agree that the classic Bishojo games are going through a state of decline (blame an oversaturated market and rampant game pirating—the downside of computer-literate consumers). But a whole new era is dawning. The race is on to deliver the Next Big Thing: cell phone Gal games. Early experiments with faux email messages from imaginary women have been promising, and frightening. There are stories of Customer Support phones besieged by desperate callers. Men who originally signed up for a game have become stalkers with no one to stalk.

Back at Furukawa Denki, I stand shoulder to shoulder with the customers, as businessmen and textbook nerdy otaku alike scour the shelves for new products, of which there are many. No one dares to make eye contact, least of all me. Even the staff seems to have blinders on as they wrap up the night's purchases in sinister black plastic bags. Presumably, everyone goes home happy for a night of fun and games. ⮧

Taito Station
See map p. 141

My favorite video game of all time has got to be The Keisatsukan, a gun game where you are a hot-dog cop who cleans up the Japanese underworld one bullet at a time. An export version, called Police 911, has begun to leak into the States, but only at Taito Station in Shinjuku is it possible that someone missing a finger might lean over and utter menacingly, "You like shooting yakuza, huh?"

Thanks to home consoles and PC gaming, coin-operated video arcades in the USA aren't what they used to be. Having thrown away countless quarters and tokens, I miss having a massive public arena to show off my button-mashing and trigger-pulling skills. Happily, Tokyo still has a booming arcade culture. You can find video arcades all over the place, usually near transportation hubs.

When I'm in Shinjuku with a few extra ¥100 coins to burn, I like to throw them away at one of the area's nicest arcades, the Taito Station. It's big, there's a good mix of demographics, there's a replica painting of Botticelli's *Three Graces* to add a touch of "class," and there's a heavenly odor from a crepes stand on the first floor. And while the atmosphere is still reminiscent of a "family fun center," the games have evolved way beyond Mr. Do! and Street Fighter II.

Any decent Japanese arcade will offer a variety of anime-derived games, such as the Lupin III shooting game, the Fist of the North

Star punching game, Mobile Suit Gundam simulators, even a Golgo 13 sniper game so difficult that you need to be a world-class hit man to get a decent score.

And the amusements include not only video games but slot machines, virtual horse racing, and Print Club photo sticker devices. Simulations that don't focus on death and mayhem are big and have done a lot to bring a wide range of people back to the arcades. Odds are, you probably know about Dance Dance Revolution, but there's also the Taiko drumming game and the samurai sword simulator to master. At any given moment, Taito Station is thus packed with tourists, local folk, families, businessmen, game freaks, gamblers, and even rougher trade.

Another big draw at any Japanese arcade—Taito Station included—are the UFO Catchers; a variation on the old "drop the crane, and try to catch the toy" gambit. Only now, the goods inside have gone from cheap stuffed toys to elaborate figures. From makers like Banpresto come fantastic 12" Godzilla figures, limited-edition *Evangelion* girls in Santa Claus suits, and plush toy versions (AKA "Plushies") of idol singers from Morning Musume. They're called UFO Catchers because the crane is said to resemble an extraterrestrial spaceship. I think they're called that because the odds of your winning something are about as rare as having a close encounter of the third kind.

But don't worry. You can always cut to the chase straight away and go to Mandarake to buy the prizes minus the pressure. ₴

Site: http://www.taito.co.jp/shisetsu/space/44.html

Sega Joypolis
See map p. 141

Half the time in Tokyo, I feel like what I'm seeing has got to be virtual reality. That being the case, it figures that the locals need something a little stronger. And as if the entire glittering fake landfill city of Odaiba weren't enough, now there's the Sega Joypolis to offer corporate-strength digital hallucination.

The power-mad dream of any great entertainment company is to someday open its own amusement park. Since Sega already had a Mickey Mouse of sorts with company mascot Sonic the Hedgehog, the eventual construction of the three-story Joypolis should come as no surprise.

It's a digital-age Disneyland, low on actual coin-op arcade machines but big on "Totally Extreme" virtual-reality amusements like skydiving, snowboarding, and river rafting. There's also the Speed Boarder, the world's first sideways roller coaster. An anime and manga influence is felt strongly courtesy of Intial D car-racing games and other 2D properties like Mushiking. Along with seasonal attractions, Joypolis even offers seasonal foods like traditional red bean cakes and pickles sold in Sonic-approved packaging.

While Joypolis attracts die-hard Sega fans from around the globe, it's not necessarily an otaku hangout per se. Real Japanese gamers might prefer something a little more "hardcore" (think Bishojo games), and

everything at Joypolis is geared around family fun. Heck, you could even bring a date here, provided he/she doesn't mind wearing those colossal VR goggles.

As I mentioned elsewhere, Joypolis makes its home in Odaiba, an artificial island built on Tokyo Bay. Constructed out of landfill in 1851, at the end of the shogun era, Odaiba (conceived as an island fortress to ward off pesky American armadas) became in the mid-'80s a massive redevelopment plan backed by the Tokyo government. But as the bubble economy collapsed, so did the grand design for a utopian City of Tomorrow. The trendy Fuji-TV network set up its headquarters there and began to tirelessly promote Odaiba as the new, hip place to hang out. The plan worked . . . but only to a point. While a famed Ferris wheel, an artificial beach, and Vegas-like shopping arcades with Italian and Chinatown themes have brought in the crowds, vacant buildings are still peppered about.

Maybe that's the best thing about the Sega Joypolis: the illusions that linger on even when you walk out the door and don't cost a thing to enjoy. ⮑

Site: http://sega.jp/joypolis/tokyo_e.html (English page)

Pachinko Parlors

Maybe because of the lack of Native American people, there are no real casinos in Japan. Nevertheless, you can gamble just about anywhere. You'll find pachinko parlors, and Japanese slot machine arcades, on nearly every street. Even if you are not all that interested in gambling, you probably still won't be able to resist dropping in on a pachinko parlor. Pictures of girls drawn in anime style will seduce you from countless banners and posters. Inside, you will see hundreds of pachinko machines lined up in rows. Many of the machines' design schemes are based on anime like *Gatchaman* (AKA *Battle of the Planets*), *Lupin the 3rd*, *Mobile Suit Gundam*, and *Space Battleship Yamato*. Animation plays in a small video monitor installed in the center of each machine. The sounds of the machines in action include memorable lines of dialogue spoken by the original anime voice actors. In short, you can gamble and watch your favorite anime at the same time! You might even make a living doing it.

But the payouts here are not Vegas-sized. The law limits the maximum jackpot amount to $200–$350. But if you hit one jackpot, you have a chance to hit a whole stampede of jackpots, a phenomenon known as *renchan*. This will keep the money coming until closing time. Some professional pachinko players (*pachi-puro*) can earn up to $1,200 a day.

There are two kinds of machines. One is the traditional pachinko machine, and the other is the pachi-slo. The pachi-slo looks more like an American slot machine, but the play is complicated and I don't recommend it for beginners.

Regular pachinko machines look like vertical pinball machines with small video monitors in the center. As in pinball, silver balls are launched into the playing area, but the balls here are only 3/8" in diameter. The balls also double as a form of currency. You buy 30–50 balls for

an enthusiastic "You will win, sweetheart!" Ah, you lucked out and matched all three items?

Congratulations! The big gate in the machine opens with great fanfare. Now the climax known as "Fever" begins. Keep on shooting all the balls you have toward the gate. You'll be rewarded with 15 balls for every ball that gets in. Soon, your plastic tray will be overflowing. Anime girls appear on the monitor again, this time dressed in bikinis and shaking their butts. And if you barely missed the jackpot? The girls will comfort you: "It was so close. . . . You almost won! Don't give up!"

The bottom line is: choose a good machine. The probability of hitting the jackpot depends on the frequency of rounds played. If you play for a while but are not winning any balls, better move on.

With a good machine, you'll hit the starter every thirty seconds, and the slot action never stops. Keep in mind that the ball shooter fires so rapidly that your ¥1,000 could be gone in less than five minutes.

Even then, your favorite anime girl will appear and try to comfort you: "This isn't your fault! Don't blame yourself. Try again, my darling!" ⏎

—By Tomohiro Machiyama

¥1,000 ($10) and put them in a tray at the base of your machine. Now twist the handle to release the balls into the playing area. They'll shoot out as fast as two per second like they were being fired by a machine-gun. The balls then drop like pinballs inside the machine and bounce around, glancing off fenders and banging into switches and jumpers. When a ball lands in a lucky pocket, the machine returns 8 to 15 balls. One of these pockets activates the video monitor. Line up two symbols and a drum roll starts playing, and an anime girl appears to cheer you up with

Talking pictures, old and new
in TokyoScope. Where to watch
them and where to collect them
for your home theater.

MOVIES

MOVIE THEATERS

Japan is infamous for its expensive ticket prices. Thanks to price-fixing by a cartel of movie theater chains, you can expect to pay as much as $20 per ticket at a mainstream cinema. Even so, most theaters in Tokyo are very old with no luxuries like stadium seating.

Still, there are some only-in-Japan perks to be had. The best one, for me, is being able to buy beer at the concession stand and drink it during the movie, even if the feature is a kiddie anime like *Pokémon* or *Hamtaro*. Again, the down side is still the price. A pint of movie beer costs $7. The other good thing about the Japanese cinema is the movie programs. First-run movie theaters sell gorgeously designed booklets about the feature attraction with plenty of full-color photos. They make a perfect souvenir for your trip.

Here are some unique theaters you cannot find in any place but Tokyo. They also make good spots for otaku-minded moviegoers to visit.

Akihabara Oriental Comic Theater

http://orient-com.jp/
03-3833-7700: Close to Suehirocho Station on the Ginza Line

Though the name makes it sound like a comedy theater, this is a brand-new

theater designed exclusively for anime screenings. And what a place to set up shop: right in the belly of Akihabara, the otaku town. The 105-seat theater has both regular 35mm film and DLP projectors, so it can show digital works. The programming is original and hard-core, like a Studio Gainax 20th Anniversary celebration, a Gundam 25th Anniversary party, and a Sakura Wars festival. Anime-related events are also frequently held here. There are lectures by directors, autograph signings by voice actors, and discussions with other otaku. You could call it "Comiket every day."

(From left) Posters for *Showa Sankyoden* (1965), *Kenkei Tai Soshiki Boryoku* (AKA *Cops Vs. Thugs*, 1974), and *The Hissatsu* (1984).

Laputa Asagaya
03-3336-5440: Asagaya Station on the JR Sobu Line

This is another theater with a strange name (in Spanish it means "The Whore"), but it is actually named for the original title of Hayao Miyazaki's 1986 anime film *Castle in the Sky: Laputa*. As the name suggests, the theater was built by a dedicated Miyazaki fanatic a decade ago. In the beginning, it played Miyazaki and Studio Ghibli masterpieces, like *Puss 'n Boots*, *Grave of the Fireflies*, and *Panda! Go Panda!*, along with some European art animation. However, recently the theater has been going in for more cinematheque-style programs, like Ozu, Kurosawa, and old Japanese black-and-white movies.

Asakusa Shin Gekijo
03-3336-5671
Asakusa Meigaza
03-3841-3028: Asakusabashi Station on the Metro Ginza Line

Asakusa, the oldest entertainment district in Tokyo, was originally established more than 200 years ago. The first motion picture theater in Japan was here, too. Sadly, just like a downtown area in rural small town America, Asakusa does not make it easy to find many remnants of its old glory days. But we love this place because it still has a couple grindhouse movie theaters. These two sixty-year-old theaters play only Japanese *jidai-geki* ("period films") and yakuza movie triple features. If you enjoyed the movies referenced in Tarantino's *Kill Bill*, like *Lady Snowblood*, you should really check these theaters out. Just be prepared for the audience: drunken old men smoking and flirty sixty-year-old transvestites.

Kabuki-cho Koma Gekijo Square
Shinjuku Kabuki-cho

This is the Japanese version of London's Leicester Square: ten movie theaters packed into one small area. Most of them do all-night shows every day. If you miss your last train home, at least you can watch a movie or sleep in a comfortable seat in an air-conditioned theater until morning comes. I once saw a 3 a.m. showing of *Spirited Away* here. It was an amazing experience watching an anime about a massage parlor in a part of Tokyo that's home to a thousand massage parlors! ⮒

–By Tomohiro Machiyama

Abeno Stamps & Coin
See map p. 141

The first time I ever went to Jinbocho Ward, I found an oversized lobby card from the Village People's flop 1980 film *Can't Stop the Music* abandoned on the sidewalk. I can't imagine too many other places on Planet Earth where something like that might happen. Jinbocho is where many of Japan's publishing companies, such as Shogakukan and Shueisha, make their home. And it's also a haven for independently run stores that sell used books, magazines, and all imaginable forms of paper and print goods.

It's easy to get lost and spend the whole day trolling the alleys, sifting through piles of dusty books looking for buried treasure. But if you've only got a few hours to spend, head for the Kanda Kosho Center Building. From near-priceless antique tomes to idol magazines from the '80s, it's all in there somewhere.

And if you've come to Tokyo with half a mind to snap up some movie memorabilia, go straight to the sixth floor and check out Abeno Stamps & Coins. Don't let the name fool you. The real specialty is movie memorabilia. This small store contains a terrifying amount of film posters, programs, lobby cards, photos, and other celluloid knockoffs.

Unlike other stores, the staff here will not jump up and shout, "*Irrashai!*" ("Welcome!") when you enter the door. The odds are they'll be content to ignore you until you actually tell them what you're looking for: promotional materials for *AKIRA*, a yakuza movie poster, the Japanese pamphlet for Hammer's *Horror of Dracula*, an adjoining lobby card set, and anything they've got on actress Meiko Kaji. Or you can browse at your leisure through enormous boxes full of goodies and piles of posters.

Then again, you can simply keep your eyes peeled as you walk down the street. You never know what you'll find in Jinbocho. ⮐

Address: Kanda Kosho Center, 6F 2-3, Kanda Jinbocho, Chiyoda-ku, Tokyo
Tel: 03-3264-2566

Video Market
See map p. 141

Every time I go to Video Market, I feel like I've finally died and gone to cult-movie heaven. Instead of a choir, there's the sound of Bruce Lee's fist connecting with a stuntman's face. Instead of the pearly gates, there are thousands of giant clamshell VHS video cases. Instead of a glowing throne where Our Heavenly Father resides, there's a multistory, mind-blowing building full of not only rare Japanese films and video but shocking and bizarre surprises from around the world.

The basement and first floor of Video Market make up a store-within-a-store called Pop Beat that sells collector's CDs (read: bootlegs), a racket that's still doing well in Japan in spite of the rise of MP3s and Internet downloads. But movie maniacs will want to rush the elevator, or jolt up the flier-strewn stairwell, to the next level.

On the second floor is Video Market's awe-inspiring Horror/Sci-Fi/Trash & Cult Movies section, a tornado of new and used DVD and VHS tapes where Mexican sleaze like *Muchachos de Barrio* rubs shoulders with Spaghetti Westerns like *The Fighting Fist of Shanghai Joe* and where low-brow zombie delegates from countless countries wait to greet, and possibly eat, you.

Where does the insatiable demand for such a variety of movies come from? As early adopters of the first commercial videocassette recorders, the Japanese have always been hungry for something to watch. During the VCR boom of the '80s, companies like JVC and Sony imported movies like *Cannibal Holocaust* and *Invasion of the Blood Farmers* by the hundreds. And the rise of the DVD is starting the cycle all over again.

More trash-as-treasure waits on the fourth floor, the domain of what Video Market calls "Asian Mondo." Here are Hong Kong flicks both new and old (with a whole lot of shelf space occupied by Bruce Lee imitators and *One-Armed Boxer* spin-offs), Bollywood musicals, and near-toxic South Korean kids' films like *Super Batman* and *Mazinger V*.

Somewhere within this maelstrom, Japanese

cult film manages to represent itself in the form of old anime, superhero, and monster tapes, along with yakuza movies, crazy sexploitation, and biker flicks.

While Video Market may proudly proclaim its affinity with "trash" from the outset, be advised that it don't come cheap. An out-of-print videocassette like Watari Tetsuya's 1973 hardboiled crime pic *Gokiburi Deka (Cockroach Cop)* can go as high as $60, and import DVDs can sell for double what they do at US chain retailers like Best Buy.

The big switch to DVD means that there are some good deals to find on old VHS tapes (I'm currently buying up old "how to play pachinko" videos to feed my VCR), but the prices on the rare and good stuff just keep rising higher and higher.

In fact, the only film genre that's seen a massive drop in price is adult video, a market where competition is fierce. Happily, floors four and five of Video Market are dedicated solely to AV, which comes in flavors far too exotic to mention here. ℮

Address: 7-9-13 Nishishinjuku, Shinjuku-ku, Tokyo
Tel: 03-3369-6613
Site: http://park11.wakwak.com/~videma/

Shopping
Prices estimated in US$

Cockroach Cop (Gokiburi Deka)
Dirty Harry, Japanese-style. Out-of-print VHS. $60 from Video Market.

Shameless School (Harenchi Gakuen)
Out-of-print VHS raunchy comedy based on Go Nagai's manga. $38 from Video Market.

Flier for Kenka Professional (AKA Black Fist)
1975 Blaxploitation "classic." $2.50 from Abeno Stamps & Coin.

Showakan News
Theater schedule for October 1934. $12 from Abeno Stamps & Coin.

COSPLAY

Costume play. Stop watching anime and BE it. Dress up as your favorite character for fun or profit.

COS-PLAY

JAN KUROTAKI
The Queen of Cosplay

I'm at a Thai restaurant in Jinbocho having a mango curry with one of the most beautiful women I'm ever likely to sit down with: Jan Kurotaki. Everyone who passes by the table glares at me like "What's she doing with that yo-yo?" and I'm starting to wonder myself. But this is strictly business. Jan is a professional cosplayer (i.e., she gets paid to dress up like anime and game characters) and a model. But she's a dojinshi author, a columnist for multiple magazines (including Animerica *in the USA). She speaks English like a Valley Girl and is without a doubt the hardest working otaku I know. The life of an international cosplay superstar is a busy one, and Jan has to leave before the food gets cold. But she's agreed to do it. She's going to write something for the book. Months later, she delivers the innermost secrets of cosplay. Enjoy. —Patrick*

This is Jan Kurotaki. And here you were thinking it was just another a cat-maid.

My name is Jan Kurotaki. I'm a cosplayer. I've loved Shonen manga, Japanese comics made for a male audience, all my life. But it's only been seven years now since my first cosplay baptism.

After thirteen years of living overseas, I finally came back to Japan. A classmate in my twelfth-grade class showed me what I had been missing out on. Somehow, even through the stress of studying for my college-entrance exam, I found acceptance both as a university student—and as a cosplayer.

Now I do have a normal job on weekdays, but on weekends, my agent and friends call me up. I put on a costume. It can be work or a party. Sometimes it can be both at the same time.

To most Japanese, ten years ago, cosplay was about wearing China dresses, nurse outfits, and other uniforms to sexually appeal to men (I hear cheerleader and policewear are popular in the States, so I think you get the point). Nowadays, it's more of a fun activity for pop-culture fans to disguise themselves as their favorite characters.

"Cosplay" is an abridgment of two words: "costume" and "player." It describes how a fan can role-play as a character by wearing a look-alike costume.

Sounds crazy, doesn't it? Yes, I admit it. We do look crazy.

It was freaky for me at my first comic convention, watching boys and girls dressing up as characters from a two-dimensional world.

Their costumes were outrageous. Enamels, leathers, and velvet dresses. It looked a hundred times more expensive than a simple witch's robe for Halloween. Girls in boys' costumes, guys in girls' costumes. Blue wigs for Rei Ayanami from *Evangelion*, yellow hair for Sailor Moon.

I definitely didn't see these people around my block. Where do these people get these costumes? Where do they come from? And most of all, why do they dream about becoming anime and manga

characters? They can't be real! The only real characters are on paper and on TV!

I gradually found out the answers from attending several cons. Fans make their own costumes, or buy them through the Internet. Most cosplayers have never sewn before in their life, but somehow pick up the skills out of love and desire.

Japanese otaku love to expand on their interests, and explore inside a hobby world. Many start from drawing and playing Nintendo, and then they shift to dojinshi, to cosplay, to making model garage kits, to photography, or even to making their own PC games.

Somehow, an otaku knows an otaku when they meet. I think there's a sixth sense we all have. Maybe that's how my friend who took me to my first con knew I would learn to love cosplay.

Cosplayers just want to express their devotion. They feel like a physical part of the world of what they love when they dress up as a character.

The more time and money you spend on your costume, the more people will admire you at events and cons. You might even begin to think you really have become the

Normal people who just pass by the venue, like families or couples with no otaku interests, see a shocking site.

Cosplay began at the largest and most famous convention for all anime and manga lovers, Comic Market (Comiket). Held twice a year, in August and December, Comiket started out as a place for self-publishers to meet and sell their goods. Originally, cosplay was just a sidedish. The first few cosplayers appeared there around the mid-'80s, and it was the only place that fans dressed up in public.

Now, Comiket is the cosplayer's "Paris Collection." We choose our very best costumes or pick a rare character to help stand out from the crowd.

Cosplay started to grow rapidly in the '90s, to the point where cosplayers began to attend smaller dojinshi events. Visual J-Rock bands emerged slowly, and fans of these artists started cosplaying as their favorite artists in Harajuku, the mecca of new fashion, every Sunday. This might have been the first exposure of real fan cosplaying to the non-otaku world, and it spread the word "Gothic-Lolita" among fashion and music lovers.

In the late '90s, the first cosplay-only event was held. It was called Tokyo Cosplay Character Show and was started by a group of amateur cameramen. The event was a blast, and over a thousand people

character at last.

When I started going to cons, I was already writing and drawing dojinshi. But cosplay was totally new to me. It hit me hard. Soon, it took over all of my spare time.

There are countless cosplay conventions and parties in Tokyo. Every week for sure, even three in a single day sometimes. However, the dates and places are only known by cosplay fans who read cosplay magazine and websites. Cosplayers in Tokyo can pick and choose which event they want to attend and enjoy.

crowded into a small hall every weekend to show off and take pictures. Now, the event continues to run twice a month, with more than two thousand regular attendees.

Soon, amusement parks in Tokyo realized how huge this trend was becoming. "Cosplay Days" have since become regular events at parks like Korakuen, Toshimaen, and Yomiuri Land in Tokyo, usually on Sundays.

Cosplayers love these amusement park cons for their huge locations and beautiful, fantasy-like scenery. Unlike at some cons, weapons and props can be freely displayed at these events, and normal folks who have no idea of what's happening also enjoy the surprise of seeing cosplayers on parade.

From these huge, unrestricted events, cosplay has become more and more open to regular society and is spreading internationally. Now that cosplay is becoming something cool and popular, people who before hid their interest are becoming free to talk about what they love. Magazines about cosplay and Gothic Lolita fashion are sold in major bookshops, and over a hundred Internet cosplay shops are desperately filling orders for new costumes.

The stereotype of the typical young otaku is someone who is isolated and shy. But that's changing rapidly thanks to cosplay: a very vivid way to express oneself.

I should know. That's how it worked out for me. ⏎

—By Jan Kurotaki

Café Mailish
See map p. 83

A dour-looking young man sits in a café surrounded by beautiful girls in ornate anime costumes. Instead of ogling them, he plays with his cell phone and drags on a cigarette. He only takes a bite or two of the strawberry shortcake he's having and then shuffles over to the register where a girl dressed like the dog-demon Inuyasha tells him cheerily to "please come back again soon." At least a dozen more guys just like him still sit in the café, lost in impenetrable thoughts. It looks like a casting call for an otaku version of *Taxi Driver*. Minus the staff and clientele, Café Mailish, located on the outskirts of darkest Akihabara, could be a classic '50s American hamburger joint, right down to the stainless steel mixers and swivel-top counter seats. Heck, you'd expect the Fonz and a pimply Ron Howard to come bouncing in.

But the soda jerks here aren't guys named Al who insist that you "try the fish." Nope. Mailish is operated by beautiful young girls wearing elaborate fantasy costumes. For the afternoon shift, classic French maid uniforms are standard attire. Then, from five until closing time, the gals trade in their black-and-white duds for colorful anime cosplay. Amuro Ray from *Mobile Suit Gundam* served me lemon tea. The girl running the cash register was a cuter version of Rurouni Kenshin (AKA Samurai X), right down to a crimson scar across her face.

You might think this is the Japanese answer to Hooters, but you'd be wrong. While American girls don the tacky shorts and tops for the money, the ladies of Mailish are genuinely into cosplay and are getting paid to do what they love. Mailish is frequented by dictionary-definition otaku: young adult males fresh from Akihabara shopping sprees, deep in the mysterious grips of *moe* (see pp. 50–51). You'd figure that in a place like this an attractive member of the opposite sex wouldn't last sixty seconds without some meatball all hopped up on Gal games harassing her. But, when asked, the cosplaying Kenshin swears that the men who come here are harmless. No one has ever tried to exchange a phone number, let alone much in the way of substantial eye contact. What little social interaction there is in Mailish happens almost by accident.

The girls, already in character and working under fake names, serve coffee and cake from the furthest reaches of fantasy. The latest service includes spoonfeeding, with the added service of having the girl blow on the food first if it's too hot for baby. Mailish also sells exclusive goods that depict the staff as big-eyed anime characters.

Those seeking a small dose of reality in Mailish will find it conspicuously absent from the menu. The lemon tea is pretty good though.

Update: When I first went to Mailish in late 2003, cosplay cafés were still a novelty and only a few existed. In the span of about six months, dozens more have sprung up in Akihabara. And while no one at Mailish was all that talkative, the setup now is more like a hostess club, where the girls sit down with you to socialize. The topic of conversation invariably turns to anime—to the point where non-otaku will not be able to keep up with the extremely knowledgeable cosplay girls. Better brush up on your Japanese and anime knowledge if you want to score. ⮐

Address: FH Kyowa Square Building 2F, 3-6-2 Sotokanda, Chiyoda-ku, Tokyo
Tel: 03-5289-7310
Site: http://www.mailish.jp/

Kigurumers
Beyond the Valley of the Cosplay Dolls

Dressing up like your favorite characters seems like a natural spin-off of anime and comic conventions.

Even so, there are people in Japan who aren't satisfied merely by wearing anime costumes. For whatever reason, they need to get inside the character's body. These people are known as "Kigurumers." (*Kigurumi* is the Japanese word for a person who wears a character mascot costume to greet customers at amusement parks or department stores.)

Kigurumers make a character costume. Then they make a face mask to go with it. Not an inch of actual skin is shown to the outside world. Since some Kigurumers cover their faces in layers of cloth, there's a risk of asphyxiation. It's a very dangerous sort of play, like bondage.

http://seriaya.hp.infoseek.co.jp/

The mostly-male Kigurumers might be seen merely as cross-dressers. But the visual strangeness of the fetish makes them even more far out than regular gender-benders. Simply by playing dress up, Kigurumers cross the boundary from fantasy to real life, from 2D to 3D, and they break a host of other taboos as well.

Some Kigurumers claim that the mask is not there to hide their face. People sublimate themselves inside the costume to act as a medium for the character's motions and thoughts. The mask is the character's head and the tights are the skin. It's a bit like playing a simulation video game. Unlike cosplayers, Kigurumers aren't wearing a costume. Rather, they physically and psychologically inhabit their characters.

If there is such as thing as an "anime lifestyle" in Japan, Kigurumers truly are its insiders. ⮌

—By Jay Tack

COMIKET

Load up on cash and take
the subway to Odaiba. It's time
for the biggest anime and manga
event in the world: Comic Market.

COMIKET 65
Tokyo Big Sight
December 28–30, 2003

It's early November 2003. I'm in Tokyo with Tomo researching life, love, and the pursuit of "liberty shops" in the Anime City. My brain cells are deteriorating from overexposure to manga, anime, and video games. Heck, I'm even considering doing cosplay, if only to try and impress Jan Kurotaki. In other words, I'm approaching a state of burnout.

Tomo senses my weakness and (in typical Tomo fashion) decides it's a good time to provoke me. He starts saying with annoying regularity, "You can't call yourself a real otaku unless you go to Comiket!" I tell him the truth: I'm near broke. The airfare, the hotel, the constant shopping sprees at Nakano Broadway and Akihabara have done me in.

This gets him off my back for a bit, but he'll keep repeating it like a mantra until I hear the words echoing on a subconscious level: "You can't call yourself a real otaku unless you go to Comiket!"

Back in the States a few weeks later, I start to get restless. After selling various parts of

my soul, along with some of my recent Tokyo haul on eBay, it's in lockdown: I'll be in Japan again from Christmas to New Year's. Maybe I'm just feeling nostalgic for Tokyo, the taste of the McTeriyaki Burger, and the company of friends. Or maybe, just maybe, I need to see the mythic beast "Comiket" for myself.

Comiket, whose name is an abbreviation of "Comic Market," is the otaku multiverse made real: a three-day pile-up of all possible Japanese subcultures at once. For the sake of brevity, you can think of it as a convention. But that's a bit like calling Woodstock "a concert."

The truth is, Comiket is more like a self-contained city-state that springs up at Tokyo Big Sight in Odaiba twice annually during summer and winter. Some 300,000 people are estimated to attend each session, making it one of the largest gatherings of people in the world.

The big draw for Comiket is dojinshi, which are limited-edition fan-made publications, usually in the form of comics but also increasingly as floppy discs or CD-ROMs known as "dojin soft." Their subject matter is often a parody of, or an erotic take on, a popular anime or manga property like *Naruto* or *One Piece*. But a million other subjects and topics are covered in the non-manga dojinshi margins, from chatter about live-action superheroes to obsessive dissertations on canned soft drinks. Production values for printed goods range from crudely Xeroxed 'zines to squarebound books with glossy covers. Dojin soft can contain anything from simple illustrations, to cosplay pictures, to original and fully playable video games. An individual either makes a dojinshi on his or her own, or as part of a clan of artists called a "circle." Some 10,000 dojin circles are crammed into the Tokyo Big Site exhibition halls. And massive as the place is, the walls can barely contain them all. Attendee lines begin in the wee hours of the morning, until the doors open at 10 a.m. Then more lines begin to form inside as dedicated

otaku become determined to nab limited-edition goods. A red-hot dojin circle dojinshi can sell out of a printrun of as many as 100,000 copies. The total amount of money that exchanges hands at a single Comiket is insane: an estimated ¥1 billion (more than what is spent at the World Cup). The profit from an independently made dojinshi can be bigger than that of a manga from a major publisher.

This great gathering of tribes may have begun as a purely fan-driven movement in 1975, but the corporations, sensing big money, have now moved in and set up their own special section. By all accounts, a kind of order has since come to Comiket. The mind reels at what the early chaotic years must have been like.

The second I get out of the subway train in Odaiba, the enormity of Comiket 65 must be confronted. There are two massive columns of moving people, and I risk being flattened in the stampede unless I become one of them. One column is headed to the nearby Comiket site, the other leads straight back toward the trains. All day, the amount of people going to and fro remains constant, like ants making work of an unsupervised picnic.

Inside the picnic basket are four massive halls brimming with activity. Navigation would be all but impossible if not for the purchase of the Comiket catalog, a three-pound phonebook-thick guide to all 35,000 dealers. Comiket regular Jan Kurotaki tells me that hardcore fans buy their catalogs days in advance, rip out pertinent pages, and form packs to better scoop up the most sought-after dojinshi with military precision. In a war zone like this, basic survival needs often take a back seat. The massive lines spread to the bathrooms as well as to the food and drink vendors at the site. Later, I'm glad I packed some snacks along with some water in my bag, which is rapidly filling up with dojinshi. Aspiring otaku that I am, I plan on spending my two days at Comiket trying to get a taste of everything. But while large chunks of the floor are devoted to a single theme (dojinshi inspired by *Shonen Jump* titles, for instance), I find out fast that I've set myself up for an impossible task. *It is totally impossible to see everything at Comiket.* After accepting this, I'm content to speed browse as many dealer's tables as I can and sample anything that looks interesting.

Comiket itself is free to attend, but to show up without any money to spend would be crazy. The ATM machines give out early on, and buying dojinshi is a cash-only affair. So it's best to bring as much dough as you feel comfortable carrying. Begging dealers for a bargain isn't considered cool, but you never know when fortune will strike on its own. For instance, I gushed like a fanboy when I stumbled across old-time erotic comic artist Dirty Matsumoto at his table, and he was compelled to throw in a few freebies after I paid him due respect. Occasionally, you'll see a cosplay girl hawking her photo CD or trying to steer people toward a particular booth. But the real action is outside in a roped-off square: the designated cosplay zone and the only place at Comiket you are technically allowed to take pictures. Hundreds of people are packed into a small roped-off space, and it looks something like Halloween in San Francisco's Castro District right before they call the cops in.

Comiket is loosely organized around themes. December 29 is Women's Day, when a good deal of dojinshi is devoted to "yaoi" works, a Slash Fiction–like genre in which graphic sex often takes a back seat to burning passions between popular male characters.

The roles are reversed on the 30th: Boys' Day. An immense sea of porn stretches out as far as the eye can see, much of it far more explicit than what you'd find in Akihabara. Alarmingly, it's the most popular section of Comiket. You can

hardly move for the size of the crowds. Suddenly, it looks like *Lord of the Rings: The Return of the King*, with mangy guys wielding backpacks full of dirty dojinshi instead of weapons.

Over in the West Hall, I stumble across the comforting sight of Jan Kurotaki. She's at Comiket both to sell her dojinshi and photo CD. Naturally, she's doing cosplay, this time as Chun-Li from the *Street Fighter* video game.

Seeing her makes me feel like I also came here clad in a disguise, and that maybe I'm a dilettante, despite my best efforts, in the world of dojinshi, manga, and anime. But after two days of enduring Comiket, and coming out alive on the other end, I've somehow managed to wind up leaving as the real thing. I'm a real otaku at last! ⊋

Gundam dojinshi for sale. How original.

Dojinshi Found at Winter Comiket 2003

1. Agul & Gaia
Presented by Kanransha
Category: yaoi

Magnificent art is one of the highlights of this tempestuous tale about two prominent Ultramen, filled with fighting, tears, and lovemaking on a truly colossal scale. Still, shouldn't they be fighting monsters somewhere?

2. Echo
Original Illustration Book, Vol. 4
By Kashima
www.ne.jp/asahi/kashima/echo
Category: illustration book

Comiket is full of illustrators seeking to strike a perfect combination of decadence and beauty. Some of them show a Lolita-Goth influence; others go for a hip-hop look familiar to fans of Gorillaz. With equal parts Art Nouveau and erotic-grotesque, plus the tiniest bit of funk, this is one of the few works that actually hit the target.

3. Rape Royale
By Dirty Matsumoto
www.rx.sakura.ne.jp/~dirty
Category: hentai

Dirty Matsumoto has been making erotic manga since the early seventies. His work has evolved from straightforward smut into a bold psychedelic new style. So much of hentai manga is unimaginative and badly drawn. With Dirty's new thing, you can't tell what the heck is going on half the time, but who cares? He makes sexual intercourse look like an experiment in particle collision.

4. Shapes of Love
By Studio Gimli
http://homepage3.nifty.com/~harry
Category: yaoi

This dojinshi depicts a "Very Special Relationship" between Legolas the elf and Gimli the dwarf from *Lord of the Rings*. There's no sex, per se, only a lot of longing stares and meaningful hugs. Even so, J. R. R. Tolkien must be spinning in his grave like a rotisserie chicken.

5. T.A.T.U. Two Loves
By Masuna Mizuho
Category: music
The Russian jailbait pop-group T.A.T.U. is notorious for being spiteful and unpleasant to work with. Yet this fan comic depicts the duo as innocent doe-eyed schoolgirls caught up in a delicate web of jealousy and crushes. Although the music act that inspired it is on the trash end of the cultural spectrum, the comic takes its name from, and is prefaced by, the 1894 poem "Two Loves" by Lord Alfred Douglas.

6. God is no where. God is now here.
By Hanao
http://www.occn.zaq.ne.jp/kinsei
Category: music
Incredibly stylish Radiohead dojinshi published in a slick American comic book format. The focus is on the relationship between frontman Thom York and hunky guitarist Jonny Greenwood. Lanky figures capture the rock star fantasy.

7. Fancy.soldier 11G
By Hiratori
http://sky.zero.ad.jp/~zaj17637
Category: military
The war machines, weapons, and uniforms of the Japanese Imperial Army are scrutinized in fetishistic detail with the help of two giggly girls who are having a great time on the battlefield. Incredible artwork is served up with overwhelming amounts of information. Other issues in the Fancy.soldier series are devoted to Nazi Germany, the British Army, and China.

8. BR Fan Book No. 6
Presented by Retikuru-za Mousou
www.geocities.jp./paradox3a
Category: movie
Inspired by the controversial *Battle Royale* novel, and no doubt also the 2000 film adaptation, this dojinshi presents two "what-if" stories about Junior High School students forced to kill each other until the last one remains standing. Focusing on gut-wrenching teen angst rather than graphic violence, this fan comic is better than the official *Battle Royale* manga adaptation published by a major.

9. *Go! Go! Godman*
Presented by Inoue
Category: special effects
With zero production values, shabby special effects, and a running time of five minutes per episode, the 1972 series *Godman* had to have been the worst Japanese superhero show ever. And yet, someone out there was motivated enough to produce a 100-page *Godman* bible. Highlights include an episode guide, analysis of *Godman*'s lackluster powers, monster suits, and a merchandise gallery that includes an LP featuring both *Godman* and *Superman* on the cover.

10. *Wota Mac: Mr. Mac Store Summer Vacation 2003*
By StudioMaruan
http://www.studiomaruan.com/wotamac/
Category: computers
Even though Macintosh users are a minority in Japan, Macs are still the preferred tools of choice for illustrators and graphic designers. No surprise then that this eight-page slice-of-life story set in an Akihabara Mac shop features some really nice and cutesy black-and-white artwork. The conflict inside revolves around sales of Power Mac G4s in the wake of the announcement of the G5.

11. *Book About Tasty Ramen Shops on the Way Home from Comiket (If You Still Have Some Strength Left), Vol. 3*
By Taku Onishi and "Ganbasu"
www2q.biglobe.ne.jp/~onishi/
Category: food
The title pretty much says it all. This eleven-page color-Xeroxed publication contains valuable information on noodle shops located on the long trek back to downtown Tokyo. Mouth-watering pics are served along with store information and detailed food reviews. Also includes color maps and the occasional manga illustration of a cat girl clutching a ramen bowl tightly to her chest.

12. *Retard*
By Matsutake Club
Category: hentai
Fan comics imagining hot and nasty sex between the teenaged characters from the *Neon Genesis Evangelion* anime are a dime a dozen. Few of them have titles quite as honest as this. ₴

MAP

A map of Comiket is a difficult thing. Imagine recording the history of an imaginary world that only lasts for three days at a time. But just to give you a sense of what Japan's biggest manga and anime event is like, here is a visual appetizer of what awaits you.

COMIKET

Comic Market Data

Place: Tokyo Big Sight (Ariake Tokyo Kokusai Tenji Jo)

Season: Every Winter and Summer

How to get there: http://www.bigsight.jp/english/access_e/index.html

Hours: 10 a.m. to 4 p.m.

Number of corporate booths: 130 (estimate)

Number of independent dojinshi circle booths: 35,000 (estimate)

CORPORATE BOOTHS LAYOUT
(FROM 2003 WINTER COMIKET 65)

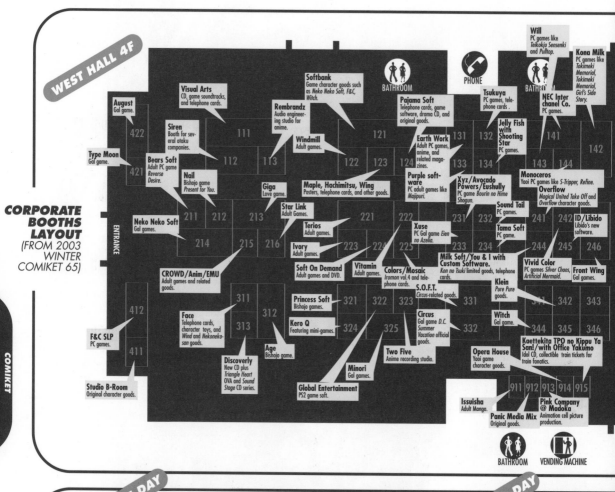

This corporate booth map is from the fourth floor of West Hall at Winter Comiket 2003. Below that is a memory map provided by Jason Thompson of San Francisco, who attended Winter Comiket in 2001. A complete map of dojinshi circles would be impossible to show here.

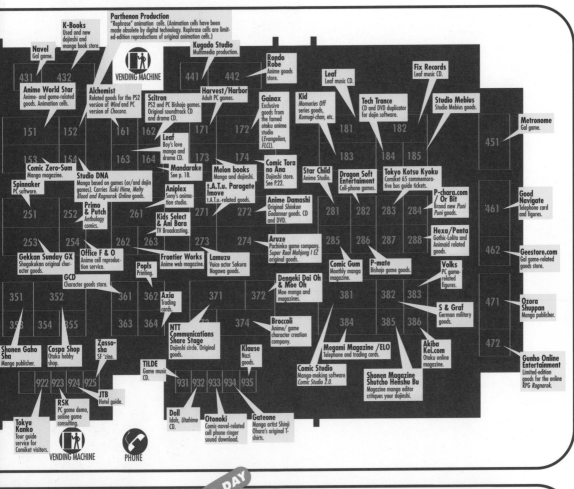

K-Books
Used and new dojinshi and manga book store.

Parthenon Production
"Rephrase" animation cells. (Animation cells have been made obsolete by digital technology. Rephrase cells are limited-edition reproductions of original animation cells.)

Kugado Studio
Multimedia production.

Navel
Gal game.

Rondo Robe
Anime goods store.

Leaf
Leaf music CD.

Fix Records
Leaf music CD.

VENDING MACHINE

431   432   441   442

Anime World Star
Anime- and game-related goods. Animation cells.

Alchemist
Related goods for the PS2 version of *Wind* and PC version of *Chocora*.

Scitron
PS2 and PC Bishojo games. Original soundtrack CD and drama CD.

Harvest/Harbor
Adult PC games.

Gainax
Exclusive goods from the famed otaku anime studio (*Evangelion*, *FLCL*).

Kid
Memories Off series goods, *Komugi-chan*, etc.

Tech Trance
CD and DVD duplicator for dojin software.

Studio Mebius
Studio Mebius goods.

Metronome
Gal game.

151   152   161   162   171   172   181   182   451

Comic Zero-Sum
Manga magazine.

Leaf
Boy's love manga and drama CD.

Comic Tora no Ana
Dojinshi store. See P.22.

153   154   163   164   173   174   183   184   185

Spinnaker
PC software.

Studio DNA
Manga based on games (or/and dojin games). Carries *Tsuki Hime, Melty Blood* and Ragnarok Online goods.

Mandarake
See p. 18.

Melon books
Manga and dojinshi.

Star Child
Anime Studio.

Dragon Soft Entertainment
Cell-phone games.

Tokyo Kotsu Kyoku
Comiket 65 commemorative bus guide tickets.

Good Navigate
Telephone card and figures.

Aniplex
Sony's animation studio.

t.A.T.u. Paragate Imove
t.A.T.u.-related goods.

P-chara.com / Or Bit
Brand new *Puni Puni* goods.

251   252   261   271   272   281   282   283   284   461

Primo & Putch
Anthology comics.

Kids Select & Ani Bara
TV Broadcasting.

Anime Damashi
Original *Shinkon Godanner* goods. CD and DVD.

Hexa/Penta
Gothic-Lolita and Animaid related goods.

Geestore.com
Gal game-related goods store.

253   254   262   263   273   274   285   286   287   288   462

Gekkan Sunday GX
Shogakukan original character goods.

Office F & O
Anime cell reproduction service.

Frontier Works
Anime web magazine.

Aruze
Pachinko game company. *Super Real Mahjong I EZ* original goods.

Comic Gum
Monthly manga magazine.

P-mate
Bishojo game goods.

Volks
PC game-related figures.

Ozora Shuppan
Manga publisher.

GCD
Character goods store.

Popls
Printing.

Lamuzu
Voice actor Sakura Nogawa goods.

Dengeki Dai Oh & Moe Oh
Moe manga and magazine.

S & Graf
German military goods.

351   352   361   362   371   372   381   382   383   471

Axia
Trading cards.

Broccoli
Anime/ game character creation company.

Megami Magazine / ELO
Telephone and trading cards.

Akiba Kei.com
Otaku online magazine.

353   354   355   363   364   374   384   385   386   472

Shonen Gaho Sha
Manga publisher.

Cospa Shop
Otaku hobby shop.

Zasso-sha
SF 'zine.

NTT Communications Share Stage
Dojinshi circle. Original goods.

Klause
Nazi goods.

Comic Studio
Manga-making software *Comic Studio 2.0*.

Shonen Magazine Shutcho Hensho Bu
Magazine manga editor critiques your dojinshi.

Gunho Online Entertainment
Limited-edition goods for the online RPG *Ragnarok*.

TILDE
Game music CD.

922 923 924 925   931 932 933 934 935

RSK
PC game demo, online game consulting.

JTB
Hotel guide.

Doll
Idols, *Utahime* CD.

Otonoki
Comic-novel-related cell phone ringer sound download.

Gateone
Manga artist Shinji Ohara's original T-shirts.

Tokyu Kanko
Tour guide service for Comiket visitors.

VENDING MACHINE   PHONE

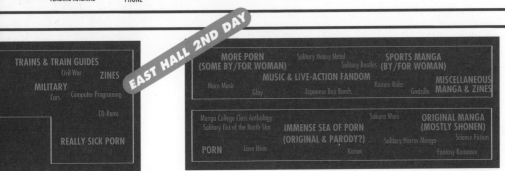

EAST HALL 2ND DAY

TRAINS & TRAIN GUIDES
Civil War
ZINES
MILITARY
Cars   Computer Programming
CD-Roms
REALLY SICK PORN

MORE PORN
(SOME BY/FOR WOMAN)
Solitary Heavy Metal
Solitary Beatles
SPORTS MANGA
(BY/FOR WOMAN)

MUSIC & LIVE-ACTION FANDOM
More Music
Glay   Japanese Boy Bands   Kamen Rider   Godzilla
MISCELLANEOUS MANGA & ZINES

Manga College Class Anthology
Solitary Fist of the North Star
Sakura Wars
ORIGINAL MANGA
(MOSTLY SHONEN)
IMMENSE SEA OF PORN
(ORIGINAL & PARODY?)
Solitary Horror Manga
Science Fiction
PORN
Love Hina   Kanon
Fantasy Romance

DOJINSHI CIRCLE BOOTH LAYOUT
(AS RECALLED BY JASON THOMPSON—OTAKU)

Most mornings while staying in Tokyo began the same way. I'd shamble out of bed, try to find some anime or superheroes on TV to help get the blood pumping, and then wander down to the nearest convenience store for coffee. Immediately, I'd find myself smack dab in a cozy oasis of otaku goodness.

Be it a store called Lawson, Family Mart, Cico Mart, or 7-Eleven, it doesn't matter. At any Japanese convenience store you'll find a fine selection of manga, toys, and video games. Best of all, most locations are open twenty-four hours day, which means you can pursue your hobby / addiction around the clock.

BREAK

Along with the usual weekly and monthly manga periodicals, there are entire lines of graphic novel collections distributed exclusively to convenience stores. While the regular bookstores get the standard-issue 200-page *tankobon* paperback collections, convenience stores offer monstrous "Super-Wide" editions that can clock in as many as 1,000 pages for a budget price of around 5 bucks.

Why bother with trying to track down a toy shop when the local am/pm has a wide selection of figures on the shelves from companies like Konami and Kaiyodo? For a few ¥100 coins, you can buy a *shokugan* (candy toy) and score a high-quality collectible figure along with a

tasty treat. Go ahead and stuff your basket with as many *Space Sheriff Gavan* Choco Eggs as you can carry in the hope of finding that one elusive limited-edition toy prize. You wouldn't be the first nerd to try.

And when you go to the cash register, you will be tempted further by the behind-the-counter selection of the latest video game, CD, and DVD releases.

What could make a plain vanilla Japanese convenience store even better? Unlike a 7-Eleven in the US, where the frozen cheeseburger will take seven to eleven years off your life, the eats at a Japanese convenience store are actually pretty good. And while the staff microwaves your tasty spaghetti bento box, peruse some manga or peek at this week's panty shots in the latest idol scandal magazine. Of course it would be great to hang out at such a fabulous place all day, but if you are actually in a hurry you can grab some fresh *onigiri* rice ball snacks and eat them on the run.

Convenience Stores

All of this makes it mighty hard to go back to the boring old convenience stores in the States, which now look to be anything but models of convenience. But take some small comfort in this fact: There are 10,000 7-Elevens in Japan, and not one of them offers a single ice cold refreshing Slurpee. ⌛

PLA-MO

Plastic model kits to build, paint, and collect (mostly collect). Be careful where you step and watch your head. Mr. Chimatsuri is inviting us inside.

CHIMATSURI

The stairs at Chimatsuri,s house. Yeah, that's right. The stairs.

Warning: This is not a story merely about old plastic model kits, how much money they are worth, and the sort of people who collect them. Rather, this is a cautionary parable about the dangers of being an otaku, the lingering effects of childhood trauma and questionable (at best) parenting, the very limits of what is permissible—not only in the country of Japan, but within the eternal darkness of the human mind itself . . . as it relates to plastic model kits.

Tokyo, early November. Winter is just beginning to creep in. It's getting cold and windy outside and the afternoon sky is cloudy and overcast. But aside from the threat of inhospitable weather ahead, it's a disarmingly peaceful day in the suburban ward of Yoga where Mari Chimatsuri (a pseudonym meaning "Blood Festival"), Japan's most notorious plastic model kit collector, has just returned home from a photo studio. The publishers of an Ultraman Encyclopedia took shots of Chimatsuri's most prized possessions for their book, which would hardly be complete without them.

Millions of Japanese kids bought the Marusan company's remote control Ultraman and Godzilla plastic model kits when they first came out in 1966 (before Chimatsuri was born). But 98 percent of the kits sold were quickly built by monster-crazed kids. Finding a single one now in pristine, unbuilt condition is akin to finding the Holy Grail. You could buy a new BMW or a Mercedes-Benz with what a single kit is worth.

Chimatsuri owns a complete set of Marusan models.

This is partially why he is in constant demand, both from other collectors and from book and magazine publishers. The other reason is that he seems to own just about every plastic model kit (known in Japanese shorthand as *plamodel*) ever made. But more about that later.

Having done his day's work (if you consider taking a bunch of model kits to a photographer work), Chimatsuri decides it's time to relax. The time is a little after 2:30 p.m. in the afternoon, but there's absolutely no reason not to drink the largest can of beer sold at the convenience store: the colossal half-gallon of Asahi. Especially when the first foreigner journalist to ever interview him is due to arrive any minute now.

Chimatsuri is clad in his standard attire. His plamodel collection may be estimated at over one million dollars, but his appearance is humble. A former construction laborer, he still adopts the classic working-class uniform: white T-shirt, wooden *geta* shoes, and a thick bath towel wrapped around his neck.

By contrast, I show up bundled in a heavy coat. I carry in my hands the standard gift one is required to bring when meeting Japan's god emperor of plastic model kits: a fresh six-pack of Asahi beer.

I figure that the interview will take place inside Chimatsuri's two-story house, which is palatial by Tokyo standards, but going inside is impossible. Part of the bottom level of the house has been converted into Chimatsuri's own plastic model kit shop. But it's also impossible to go inside there, because Chimatsuri can no longer reach the light switch anymore. That's because every square inch is smothered in model kits.

Indeed, it quickly becomes clear that Chimatsuri lives inside his plastic model kit collection. His entire house is full of them from floor to ceiling. It seems impossible in theory. But it is true. Chimatsuri invites me to take a look for himself. The entryway to the house is

guarded by enormous plastic garbage bags. They are beginning to rip and tear. They are filled with model kit boxes. Opening the front door, I'm reduced to a state of shock. Boxes of unbuilt kits are everywhere. Thousands of them. Perhaps tens of thousands of them. My eyes cannot believe what they see.

"Be careful where you step," Chimatsuri suggests.

Too late. A tidal wave of plastic model kit boxes crashes down on my head. This place is dangerous! How could anyone live here? Emerging from the pile of kits, I attempt to climb the model-kit-lined stairs. Entering the main bedroom, I begin to feel like Indiana Jones or a policeman who has accidentally stumbled across a madman's lair. There's no furniture (even a bed) or even a bare patch of space to be found. Model kits! Model kits! Everywhere!

Incredibly, Chimatsuri claims he knows exactly where every piece, valuable or otherwise, in his seemingly chaotic collection resides. One assumes that he also knows a way down the stairs without falling into a plastic model kit hell. I'd sure like to know.

After a sweat-inducing body-contorting trip down to the surface again, I need a break. I struggle to make it to the toilet. Which is, of course and quite naturally, filled with boxes of unbuilt plastic model kits.

The first formal question of the interview is obvious, but it has to be asked: "Why do you collect plastic model kits?"

The answer is not a short one. Chimatsuri has decided to take this opportunity to tell his life story, which is interrupted by cackling laughter, gulps of beer, periodical cell phone calls, and requests to repeat what he's said simply because the tale astonishes. Chimatsuri himself is as strange as his house is. Perhaps far stranger.

"When I was three years old I was first exposed to plastic models. I loved building them. What I really liked to do was build them up, and then take them apart so I could build them all over again."

Unfortunately, Chimatsuri's mother accidentally mistook all the spare parts she found one day for junk. Thinking the parts belonged to useless broken kits, she made an unfortunate decision whose repercussions she is still dealing with to this day.

"One day I came home from school and I

started seeing many plastic model parts in the street. I followed the trail and saw a huge garbage truck with all the plamodels I owned inside! See, I kept all the parts in a huge cardboard box with holes at the bottom. That's why many pieces had fallen out. All I could do was stand there and watch helplessly as they were crushed."

The shock and outrage of losing now-valuable first-generation Kamen Rider and Mazinger Z models kits becomes momentarily evident in Chimatsuri's face.

"Of course I began collecting again. But now I only cared about tanks. Nazi tanks. It was the golden age of the military model kits from the Tamiya Company, and I thought they were the only proper things a boy should build. But I couldn't get enough of making regular model kits."

Using putty, super-glue, toothpicks, and dangerous customized electrical tools, Chimatsuri began turning Tamiya models of British soldiers into Ultraman monsters. He produces one from his pocket. It is a perfect likeness of Kanegon, the money-eating monster from Ultra Q, a fitting choice considering how much cash Chimatsuri has invested in his collection. It looks

This Red King model kit originally sold for $6.50 in 1967. Today, it's worth around 10–15 grand.

nothing like a Tommy soldier. Chimatsuri's modeling talents cannot be contested. But they severely lack in one area.

"I'm terrible at painting. I never learned how," he laughs.

One day in 1979, he took a customized Nazi jeep over to a friend's house. Hoping to impress his pal, he found that his very best efforts had already been eclipsed by a mass-produced kit.

"My friend had a plamodel of a Domu mobile suit from Gundam. I'd never seen anything like it before. I asked him, 'What is it?' He said, 'Don't you know? This is from Gundam!' 'What's Gundam?' I asked, but he just laughed at me. I rushed to the nearest toy shop and told the old woman who worked there, 'Give me Gundam! I want to buy Gundam!' She said, 'What are you talking about? There's no Gundam left here!'"

The Gundam boom had exploded in Japan and all the kits were sold out. Once again, scarcity forced Chimatsuri to make a dramatic comeback.

"It was then I discovered that there were many new kinds of animation and character model kits on the market and I began collecting all of them. Up until Gundam, all I cared about was monsters and military kits."

It was now time to ask the second, and technically last question of the interview, "How did you acquire your rare Marusan monster kits?" Another beer later, the increasingly red-faced and animated Chimatsuri continued to speak.

"There is a famous toy shop called Billiken. They used to have many rare plamodel kits that were kept in a glass case. I went there for the first time when I was thirteen. I'd seen pictures of the kits before in otaku magazines like *Hobby Japan* and *Uchusen*, but never with my own eyes. I told the salesman, I'll take all of them! He couldn't believe it! But it happened. My mom bought the kits. It must have cost around three thousand dollars. It is a legendary event to this day in plamodel collector circles."

The Otaku boom of the eighties was in full bloom. Chimatsuri, who apparently came from a family with deep pockets and a lot of guilt over throwing away his old models, was in a perfect position there to reap all the benefits.

"My family had sold some valuable real estate in the countryside before moving here. I was the youngest of four kids, so I've always been spoiled," he says proudly.

Not only was a whole new wave of animation reinvigorating Japanese pop culture (as well as the bubble economy), but collectors were beginning to emerge as peculiar kinds of celebrities in their own right.

"When I was sixteen, I saw an issue of *Uchusen* magazine that featured a plamodel collector named Hirai. I wrote to him and asked if I could buy his collection. The price for everything he had was $8,000. I bought it. This is another legend."

But what does a teenage boy do once he actually owns the rarest model kits in all of Japan (and maybe even on the planet as well)?

"At first, I never wanted to touch them. That was my policy. But the tension from owning the kits and not being able to build them was driving me crazy. So I got into making replicas. You can use silicon rubber to make molds and then build those. But I never painted the copies. I can't paint."

But such a golden age could not last forever. The family was running out of money, partially because of Chimatsuri's out-of-control plamodel addiction. Desperate measures were called for.

"I became a yankee [a Japanese juvenile delinquent]. Me and my friends formed a gang and we would go to Shibuya, squat on the ground, and bother people passing by. When we saw a weak-looking salaryman, we would take his money. But we would do it without breaking the law. We wouldn't yell at them and demand things. We would ask them as politely as possible if we could borrow some money. If they said no, we would pin them up against a vending machine and punch it right next to their head. Then we would ask them politely again. They usually paid. If they didn't, then we would beat the hell out of them. As long as we didn't blackmail or threaten them, we weren't breaking the law."

Chimatsuri delivered the manifesto behind his otaku Clockwork Orange–like

existence: "Even though we were a gang, we'd watch anime on TV and we always sang the theme songs. Then we'd go out again and do bad things. We split the money we made three ways: for sake, video games, and plastic models, mostly plastic models."

Unfortunately, a car-and-motorcycle stealing spree finally led to Chimatsuri's arrest. To compound the bad luck, his family was forced to sell the house they'd lived in for twenty years. His collector habits had brought them to ruination. Once released from jail, he actually had to start working for a living.

"My eldest brother worked at Toei Studios in the optical effects department. So I got a construction job there. Every payday, I would go to an antique store in Shimokitazawa called Natsukashi-ya [Nostalgia] and buy models. Eventually, the store owner told me I should quit my job and open my own store. That way I could buy all the models I wanted at wholesale prices. I began working part-time at Natsukashi-ya so I could learn about the business. Eventually, I applied for an antique shop license. Actually, my father did because I wasn't allowed to because of my police record."

With no money left to open a full-fledged business, Chimatsuri and his father treated their house like a 1/1 scale model kit and recustomized it until they had a storefront. Sadly, his father died a month before the store, called Sailor-ya (after the traditional schoolgirl uniform) officially opened. That was ten years ago. Since then, life has been pretty good for Chimatsuri.

"I make my living now selling plamodels and writing about them."

He's coauthored several books on the history of Japanese model kits and pens a monthly column for *Figure-Oh (Figure King)* magazine. How about his domestic life?

"My mother is now seventy years old. She lives here with me and my wife. I don't give her any money. I just give her old model kits

had a wife?

"I met her ten years ago. We fell in love. The problem is that she is actually a man, but that's the only problem. Mentally, we are in love, but not physically. I'm not gay. I still love women and watch a lot of porno animation and adult videos. I don't know why it worked out like this."

I'm feeling numb now. Too many crazy things have been seen and heard. Hearing that Chimatsuri is married to a man now

(From left) The man, the myth himself, Chimatsuri, (middle) Ultraman model kits worth serious moolah, (right) No rest in the rest room.

that I don't want and she sells them."

Soon enough, an old woman comes drifting down the street on a creaky bicycle. Chimatsuri completely ignores her until she is within range. "Baba!" (old hag) he screams, and throws an empty beer can at her as she returns to the maddest house in all of Tokyo.

But wait a second. Did Chimatsuri say he

sounds like the most normal thing in the world. So does his final message.

"Please tell your readers not to come to my store unless they learn Japanese first. Foreigners who can't speak Japanese make me crazy." ↩

Sailor Ya (open from 2–9 pm, Mon–Thurs, Sun)
Address: 4-25-5 Yoga, Setagaya-ku, Tokyo
Tel: 03-3700-1394

Mondo Tokyo:
SHINJUKU

Ringo means "apple" in Japanese, so pop idol Shiina Ringo is known as the "Japanese Fiona Apple." Anyway, a few years ago, her song "Queen of Kabuki-cho" generated quite a little buzz. The lyrics go something like "My mother was the Queen of the town/I'm her spitting image/When she left me, I was only fifteen years old/I hold it against her, but I proudly declare myself Queen/The only thing I can sell is myself/If I craved someone's compassion, I would lose everything/If you come out of the east gate of Shinjuku Station, you can see my territory/Kabuki-cho, East Asia's Great Sin City."

In spite of the fact that Ringo has never worked in Kabuki-cho and has had no actual experience peddling her ass, this controversial song was a smash hit and became a karaoke favorite with female students. Some people said "Queen of Kabuki-cho" would become the town

anthem, but it didn't because the women who really worked there thought the whole song was way behind the times. A typical complaint went, "We're not orphans or losers. It's not like it's the '50s!"

Kabuki-cho is an approximately 40,000-square-meter area located at the southeast side of Shinjuku Station in west-central Tokyo. Most of the towering buildings are crowded full of *fuzoku*, sex-related businesses like massage parlors, from basement to top. The number of *fuzoku* shops is estimated at 5,700, and the number of women working there is more than 10,000.

The softest and classiest category of *fuzoku* is "Club." In Japan, "Club" means a super-gorgeous bar where super-gorgeous hostesses in super-gorgeous long dresses serve their customers. Most Clubs are concentrated around Kuyakusho-dori. You can only enjoy having a decent conversation with the women, but it's not boring:

they're so professional they read every newspaper and all recent bestsellers, so they can talk about almost any topic. The problem is, Clubs are incredibly expensive. If you spend one hour, they charge you more than ¥36,000 (around $300 nowadays).

A "Cabacla" is a cheaper version of a Club. The quality of the girls there is tolerable. Sometimes not. Conversation with them is, more often than not, hell. No wonder, since the girls make just ¥2,500 (about $20) an hour. If you want to have fun in a Cabacla, you gotta possess the ability to entertain the girls yourself. The best thing is their cheap uniform, which shows off their cleavage and features an extremely short skirt. Also, there are hardcore Cabacla, like "Lingerie Club," "Osawari (Touching) Club," and "Kiss Club", but there aren't so many of those.

The most standard *fuzoku* in Kabuki-cho are massage parlors, most of which are located at Ichibangai ("First Avenue") and Sakura-dori. The shops are classified by the image of the girls who work there: schoolgirl, college student, office worker, housewife, foreigner, etc. Some girls are in costume, but some are "real."

From this info, you might be thinking this is some dark and horrifying meat market like Sodom or 42nd Street circa '70s NYC, but Kabuki-cho is a nice, bright place. Too bright. Even after midnight, a flood of glittering neon signs wipes out any sign of darkness from the streets. Most bars and movie theaters are open all night. The streets are full of crowds of young women and teenaged girls walking around, talking perky and laughing merrily at three in the morning. They don't look like bad girls, either, just ordinary office workers and students. So it's actually a pretty safe town. However, nobody can tell which girls are just playing and which are working there.

Kabuki-cho girls are not junkies, nor are they exploited by yakuza pimps. Sure, many of them probably started their job to pay off debts, but they can freely spend all the money they earn. They are all independent contractors. The richest girls are Soap

Ladies, who offer full-service sex. They make money up to ¥160,000 ($2,000) a day.

In Kabuki-cho there are only nine Soaplands, which are lined along Nakamise-dori. I once talked to a girl named Reina, who worked in a high-class Soapland on that street. She said she'd also worked in Las Vegas for about six months. She used to do a striptease show at

Name your Kabuki-cho poison. Karaoke or the "Virtual Mirror Club Pinky" peep show.

Rock-Za, a historical cabaret theater in Asakusa, but she wanted to learn professional dancing and performance, so she flew to Vegas and got on some stages. She financed the trip herself. In addition, she had learned classic ballet when she was young, and she could speak

pretty good English. Unfortunately, I didn't listen to her story as a customer because I was there to interview her for a magazine feature about Shinjuku. She showed up for our interview decked out in a white Chanel suit she had had tailor-made in Paris. According to her, the most popular hobby of Soap Ladies is traveling and shopping. They're always going to Hong Kong, NYC, and Paris to shop at Bvlgari, Hermes, and Gucci.

As Reina put it, "The problem is that we have too much money to spend. Some of my friends are addicted to Host Clubs." "Host Club" is the opposite of Club. A Host Club is where good-looking guys serve female customers. There are a lot of huge Host Clubs in Kabuki-cho, so most of their customers are women who work in *fuzoku*! They buy their favorite hosts Rolex watches, Yohji Yamamoto suits, and even cars—all with the money they get for selling themselves.

Anyway, you might guess that, instead of "Queen of Kabuki-cho," the real theme song of Kabuki-cho girls is

Destiny's Child's "All the honeys who makin' money/Throw your hands up at me." Shortly after I interviewed Reina, though, the Japanese economy tanked. The unemployment rate is going up every day, and the situation pushes more and more girls into Kabuki-cho. That's why Shiina Ringo's song was such a hit: average girls could easily relate to a song about the "Queen of Kabuki-cho."

However, the girls I've been talking about are all Japanese, and they only work north of Hanamichi-dori. This avenue runs through the center of Kabuki-cho from east to west and acts as a kind of border between Japanese Kabuki-cho and "ethnic" Kabuki-cho. South of Hanamichi-dori is "Deep Kabuki-cho," where thousands of foreign prostitutes hang around in front of lousy hotels. They come from Thailand, the Philippines, China, Taiwan, Korea, Russia, Romania, Colombia, and Brazil. The only Japanese they can speak is "Oniisan, yasui yo" ("Sir, I'm cheap"). Once, I saw a pimp collecting his money from one of his girls in a McDonald's at midnight. This Filipino guy had a big, macho mustache and was dressed in a long leather black coat with a big black hat. He was counting his money with fingers decorated by glitter rings. I felt like I was in Harlem in the 1970s.

I don't recommend you go in that deep, because it's extremely dangerous. Nevertheless, it's still worth visiting Kabuki-cho. There are bright, gorgeous women, scary thugs, and good food from all over the world, all in one place! It's a carnival and festival every day around the clock, literally. It's just crazy.

—By Tomohiro Machiyama

All the flavors of Kabuki-cho: adult books and videos, a nurse cosplay club, a kogal bar, okonomiyaki and ramen.

MAP

A selective look at the locales in this book and how to get around Tokyo. Not a complete guide to train lines and transportation routes, but a "greatest hits" package … let's go!

JR Lines
Yamanote Line
Sobu Line
Chuo Line
Saikyo Line
Joban Line
Keihin Tohoku Line
Other JR Lines

Akabane

Matsudo

Ikebukuro — Sugamo — Tabata — Kitasenju

Nishinippori

Takadanobaba

Korakuen

Ueno — Asakusa

Shinokubo

Mitaka — Ogikubo — Nakano

Ochanomizu — Akihabara — Asakusabashi

Shinjuku

Jinbocho

Yoyogiuehara

Kanda

Harajuku

Tokyo

Shibuya

Hibiya

Ebisu

Kasumigaseki — Ginza

Meguro

Yurakucho

Yoga

Shinbashi

Osaki

Hamamatsucho — Ariyake

Shinagawa

Odaiba

Chiba

Subway
Ginza Line
Marunouchi Line
Chiyoda Line
Hanzomon Line

Others
Odakyu Line
Monorail Line
Limousine Bus
Keisei Sky Liner
Narita Express

Yokohama

Haneda Airport

Places where authors almost passed out...

Nakano
Mandarake (Manga), p. 18

Taco ché (Manga), p. 24

Nakano Broadway (Shopping Center), p. 29

Shinjuku
GeraGera Manga Café (Manga Café), p. 26

Big Echo (Karaoke), p. 64

Kabuki-cho Koma Gekijo Square (Movie Theater), p. 104

Video Market (Video Store), p. 106

Taito Station (Arcade), p. 96

Shibuya
Hello! Project Official Store (Idol Shop), p. 60

Akihabara
Tora no Ana (Book Store), p. 22

Gatchapon (Toy Store), p. 42

Map, p. 83

Akihabara Oriental Comic Theater (Movie Theater), p. 103

Café Mailish (Coffee Shop), p. 113

Jinbocho
Abeno Stamps & Coin (Movie Posters), p. 105

Odaiba
Sega Joypolis (Arcade), p. 97

Ariyake
Comiket, p. 118

Asakusa
Marubell Do (Idol Shop), p. 58

Asakusa Meigaza (Movie Theater), p. 104

Asakusa Shin Gekijo (Movie Theater), p. 104

Yoga
Sailor Ya (Toy Store), p. 137

TO THE ANIME CITY

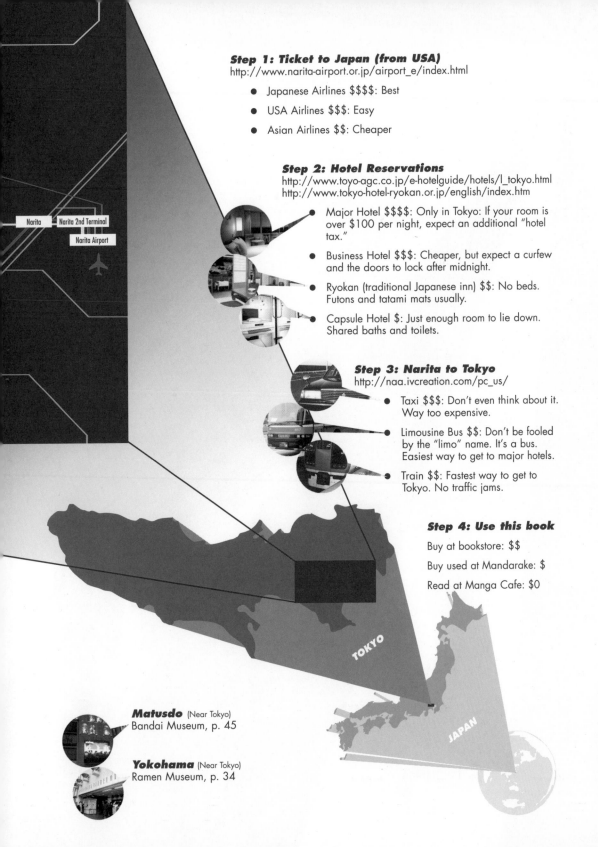

Step 1: Ticket to Japan (from USA)

http://www.narita-airport.or.jp/airport_e/index.html

- Japanese Airlines $$$$: Best
- USA Airlines $$$: Easy
- Asian Airlines $$: Cheaper

Step 2: Hotel Reservations

http://www.toyo-agc.co.jp/e-hotelguide/hotels/l_tokyo.html
http://www.tokyo-hotel-ryokan.or.jp/english/index.htm

- Major Hotel $$$$: Only in Tokyo: If your room is over $100 per night, expect an additional "hotel tax."
- Business Hotel $$$: Cheaper, but expect a curfew and the doors to lock after midnight.
- Ryokan (traditional Japanese inn) $$: No beds. Futons and tatami mats usually.
- Capsule Hotel $: Just enough room to lie down. Shared baths and toilets.

Step 3: Narita to Tokyo

http://naa.ivcreation.com/pc_us/

- Taxi $$$: Don't even think about it. Way too expensive.
- Limousine Bus $$: Don't be fooled by the "limo" name. It's a bus. Easiest way to get to major hotels.
- Train $$: Fastest way to get to Tokyo. No traffic jams.

Step 4: Use this book

Buy at bookstore: $$

Buy used at Mandarake: $

Read at Manga Cafe: $0

Narita · Narita 2nd Terminal · Narita Airport

Matusdo (Near Tokyo)
Bandai Museum, p. 45

Yokohama (Near Tokyo)
Ramen Museum, p. 34

TOKYO

JAPAN

Thanks to:
Akira Iwasaki
Alvin Lu
Andrew W.K.
Animerica
Ayumi Nakayama
Carl Gustav Horn
Clive France
Egan Loo
Eiga Hi-Ho
Fko-san
Foofer
Gen Otani
Ginty Kobayashi
Happy Ujihashi
Hawk Terasawa
Hiromi Machiyama
Hiroyuki Watanabe

Hisanori Nukada
Izumi Nishimura-Evers
Jaime Starling
Jan Kurotaki
Jason Thompson
Jay Tack
Junk Hunter Yoshida
Junko Mizuno
Kantetsu Nagata
Kiichiro Yanashita
Kyoko Uemoto Florendo
Makiko Yanagi
Manabu Mizuno
Mari Chimatsuri
Masanori Oya
Masuzo Furukawa
Million Publishing
Monica Fukusato
Naohito Tanobe
Outrageous Cherry
Peter Goodman

Princess Soft
Riki Takeuchi
Shigeru Igari
Shohei Onishi
Shota Oba
Stone Bridge Press
Takashi Miike
Takehiro Higuchi
Tetsuro Tamba
The staff of Mandarake
The staff of Sansai Books
The staff of Taco Ché
The Status Quo
Toei Animation
Toei Co. Ltd.
Video Market
Wes Black & Joseph Luster
Yosensha Publishing
Yoshiki & Maki Takahashi